The Survival Guide
for Parents
of Gifted Kids

How to understand,
live with, and stick up for
your gifted child

The Survival Guide for Parents of Gifted Kids

How to understand, live with, and stick up for your gifted child

SALLY YAHNKE WALKER

EDITED BY SUSAN K. PERRY

Free
Spirit ®
PUBLISHING

Library of Congress Cataloging-in-Publication Data
Walker, Sally Yahnke, 1942–
  The survival guide for parents of gifted kids: how to understand,
  live with, and stick up for your gifted child / Sally Yahnke Walker; edited by
  Susan K. Perry; illustrated by Caroline Price.
      p.   cm.
  Includes bibliographical references and index.
  ISBN 0-915793-28-8
  1. Gifted children—United States.   2. Gifted children—Education—
United States.   3. Parent and child—United States.   I. Perry, Susan K.,
1946–   . II. Title.
HQ773.W35   1991
649'.155—dc20

Printed in the United States of America
10 9 8 7 6 5 4 3 2 1

Cover and interior design by MacLean & Tuminelly
Illustrations by Caroline Price
Supervising editor: Pamela Espeland

FREE SPIRIT PUBLISHING INC.
400 First Avenue North, Suite 616
Minneapolis, MN 55401
(612) 338-2068

PERMISSIONS AND CREDITS

"Is Gifted Ed Elitist?" on page 11 quotes Jim Bray, "The Governor's School of North Carolina (West)," *G/C/T*, May/June 1979, No. 8, p. 57. "A Do-It-Yourself Inventory" on pages 21-22 is adapted from Van Tassel-Baska and Strykowski, *An Identification Resource Guide on the Gifted and Talented*, Northwestern University, 1988. The creativity characteristics on page 23 are adapted from Renzulli, Smith, White, Callahan, and Hartman, "Scales for Rating Behavioral Characteristics of Superior Students," Creative Learning Press. "How Kids Feel About the 'Gifted' Label" on page 27 is quoted from James Delisle and Judy Galbraith, *The Gifted Kids Survival Guide II: A Sequel to the Original Gifted Kids Survival Guide (For Ages 11-18)* (Minneapolis: Free Spirit Publishing Inc.), p. 144, and James R. Delisle, *Gifted Kids Speak Out* (Free Spirit, 1987). Information about young children on page 33 is adopted from Merle Karnes, Allan Schwedel, and Polly Kemp, "Maximizing the Potential of the Young Gifted Child," *Roeper Review*, Volume 7, Number 4, with permission of the *Roeper Review*. Information on the fears and worries of gifted children on pages 46-47 is adapted from Derevensky and Coleman, "Gifted Children's Fears," *Gifted Child Quarterly*, 33:2, Spring 1989. Suggestions for helping children deal with death on page 47 are adapted from Virginia L. Fortner, "Ask the Experts," *Gifted Children Monthly*, May 1987. The physical activities suggested on page 48 are adapted from Susan K. Perry, *Playing Smart: A Parent's Guide to Enriching, Offbeat Learning Activities for Ages 4-14* (Minneapolis: Free Spirit Publishing Inc., 1990). Information on early reading on page 52 is adapted from "Not All Gifted Kids Read Early," *Gifted Children Newsletter*, July 1980. The section, "Ten Tip-Offs to Trouble," on pages 70-74 is adapted from James Delisle, "Gifted Children's Fears," in *Gifted Children Newsletter* (now *Gifted Children Monthly*), February 1984, and "Are Gifted Girls Prone toward Eating Disorders?" from February 1987. The signs of a teen in trouble on page 74 are adapted from Miriam Adderholdt-Elliott, Ph.D., *Perfectionism: What's Bad About Being Too Good?* (Minneapolis: Free Spirit Publishing Inc., 1987). The gifted programming methods described on pages 84-87 are adapted from Judy Galbraith, *The Gifted Kids Survival Guide (For Ages 11-18)* (Minneapolis: Free Spirit Publishing Inc., 1983). The young gifted girl on page 82 is quoted from *Gifted Kids Speak Out*, p. 54. The information on gifted program differentiation in the product area is adapted from C. June Maker, *Teaching Models in Education of the Gifted* (Austin, TX: Pro-Ed, 1982), p. 220. The characteristics of gifted teachers listed on page 94 are adapted from *Gifted Kids Speak Out*, p. 80. Material quoted in "Bored No More" on page 96 is from Judy Galbraith, "The Eight Great Gripes of Gifted Kids: Responding to Special Needs," *Roeper Review* 8:1, 1985, p. 15. "Ten Tips for Talking to Teachers" on page 102 is adapted from Judy Galbraith and Pamela Espeland, "10 Tips for Talking to Teachers," *Free Spirit: News & Views on Growing Up Gifted*, Vol. 2, No. 1. Information on specific states in "How's Your State Doing?" on pages 109-110 is adapted from The Council of State Directors of Programs for the Gifted, *The 1987 State of the States Gifted and Talented Education Report*. The information on how bills are passed in the Illinois state legislature on pages 108-109, and the sample letters and telephone scripts on pages 111-113, have been adopted from the Illinois Council for the Gifted, "State Gifted Advocacy," by Dr. Trevor T. Steinbach. Suggestions for establishing rules for kids on pages 121-122 are adapted from Melvin Silberman and Susan Wheelan, *How to Discipline Without Feeling Guilty* (Champaign, IL: Research Press, 1981).

DEDICATION

To my mother,
who has always encouraged me
to be all that I could be,
and more.

ACKNOWLEDGMENTS

Thanks to Bob for the push I needed;
to Sarah, Amy and Beth for keeping me humble;
to Cyndy for her help;
to Becky for all the computer know-how;
and to all the parents I have worked with
for their ideas and inspiration.

CONTENTS

Foreword   xiii

Introduction   1

The Eight Great Gripes
of Parents with Gifted Kids   3

CHAPTER 1:
GIFTEDNESS THEN AND NOW   5

The Birth of the Word "Gifted" ★ Myths About
Giftedness ★ The Not-So-Pretty Truth About Gifted
Education ★ See-Sawing Attitudes ★ The Marland
Report ★ Progress, Finally

CHAPTER 2:
WHAT MAKES GIFTED KIDS SO SPECIAL?   15

The Curve and the Law of "Averages" ★ How Kids Are
Identified as Gifted ★ What Happens Next? ★
The Question of Labels ★ Kids Who Fall Between
the Cracks ★ Putting Things in Perspective

CHAPTER 3:
LIVING WITH YOUR GIFTED CHILD   35

Endless Questions ★ Active for a Reason ★ Remember
When? ★ Early Walkers, Speedy Talkers ★ Across the
Ages ★ The Motor Skills Gap ★ Coping with Young
Lawyers ★ The Company of Adults ★ The Importance
of Risk-Taking ★ What's So Funny? ★ Fast Learners,
Deep Learners ★ Fears and Worries ★ Sound Minds
in Sound Bodies ★ Concentration and Relaxation ★
When Neatness Doesn't Count ★ Early Readers ★
The Importance of Staying in Touch

CHAPTER 4:
COPING WITH PROBLEMS   57

How Not to Raise a Nerd ★ Dealing with Sensitivity ★
Intolerance and the Too-Smart Mouth ★ Too Good:
The Perfectionism Predicament ★ When to Worry ★
How to Get Help

CHAPTER 5:
PROGRAMMING FOR THE GIFTED   79

Gifted or "Dumb"? ★ Making School Better for Gifted
Kids ★ Your Rights and What's Right ★ Toward a Better
Curriculum ★ What Are Teachers For? ★ It's a Match!

CHAPTER 6:
ADVOCACY: WORKING FOR IMPROVEMENT 99

Advocacy on the Local Level ★ How to be Heard: Begin with the Teacher ★ Working with the School Board ★ Getting Support for Yourself ★ Getting "Them" Moving on the State Level ★ How's Your State Doing? ★ Getting Your Message Across ★ A Few Final Words

15 Questions Parents Ask—and 14 ½ Answers   115
More Recommended Reading   125
Bibliography   127
Index   131
About the Author   137

FOREWORD

EVER SINCE WE PUBLISHED *The Gifted Kids Survival Guides*, parents have asked us, "Where's *our* Guide? You're helping our kids cope with growing up gifted—we need help coping with them!"

In 1986 we published *Bringing Out the Best: A Resource Guide for Parents of Young Gifted Children* to address some of the issues of early identification and early education of gifted kids. But we were still waiting for the right book for parents of kids already in school—parents who were learning that giftedness is no guarantee of smooth sailing, good grades, emotional health, or social success.

We believe that Sally Yahnke Walker has written the right book for those parents, and anyone else who wants or needs to know more about gifted young people. Like *The Gifted Kids Survival Guides*, *The Survival Guide for Parents of Gifted Kids* offers information, advice, and a lot of encouragement. It is not meant to be a scholarly work (there are already several of those out there), although there's solid scholarship behind it. Nor is it meant to be a textbook, although parenting classes may find it useful.

What *is* it meant to be, then? It's a friendly resource—a place parents can turn to for answers to their questions about their own children. It's a book that, in the tradition of *The Gifted Kids Survival Guides*, can be skimmed or read in-depth, opened anywhere, and enjoyed. And it's a book that will help you understand that you're not alone—other parents have problems similar to yours, and no, you're *not* crazy!

So, for all those parents who have wondered, "Where's *our* Guide?"...here it is.

Judy Galbraith, President and Publisher
Free Spirit Publishing Inc.
February 1991

INTRODUCTION

NO ONE EVER SAID it would be easy to raise a gifted child, but no one ever told you it would be this hard. This parenting business can be overwhelming!

Often, whatever support you find, you have to seek out yourself. Large, close families with relatives nearby are a thing of the past, and even when there are grandparents or other relatives handy, they don't always understand what you're going through with your kid. You're likely to hear a symphony of, "Why don't you just..." or "If you'd only...." Of course, you've just tried whatever they're suggesting, only it hasn't worked. Not with your intense, precocious child. Sometimes it feels like nothing you try works and all you get is blame for your efforts.

That's when this Survival Guide can help. Think of it as your portable support service, available to answer your questions and give you a pat on the back when you need it.

WHO IS THIS BOOK FOR?

THE SURVIVAL GUIDE FOR PARENTS OF GIFTED KIDS is for every parent whose child has shown signs of unusual intelligence or talent in some area.

Maybe your child has been tested and identified as "gifted." Maybe not. Either way, you're the best judge of whether his or her needs are being met. It seems that as soon as your child steps out of the ordinary, the tough job of parenting gets even tougher. If you're wondering whether you're doing everything right, this book is for you.

WHAT IS THIS BOOK ABOUT?

THE BOOK YOU'RE HOLDING won't inform you of the latest ways to raise a prize-winning whiz kid. It won't give you ten tips on how to turn junior into a champion or get him into college at age 12.

What you will learn from this book is how and why your child is different from his or her schoolmates of more average ability. You'll discover how some of those traits sometimes lead to trouble, and what you can do about that if it happens. You'll learn a little about the history of gifted education and how school systems deal with the special needs of the gifted today. You'll read stories of other parents who have recognized and handled difficult situations with their gifted kids.

As I've worked with groups of parents of gifted and talented children, I've noticed that their questions seem to go on forever. In this book, you'll find answers to many of your questions, including some you didn't know you had. Here are a few of the issues that are discussed in these pages:

▶ Do a smart mind and smart mouth always go together?

▶ How do I deal with a daughter who's constantly pushing her limits and using logic against me?

▶ How do other parents cope with constant questions, ongoing experiments, and growing collections?

▶ How hard and how far should I push my child?

▶ What's the best education for a gifted and talented child?

▶ How can my child be "gifted" in one school and not in another? Did he lose something when we moved?

Speaking of schools, it used to be that parents were intimidated by the educational system. They were afraid to speak up for their kids. Lately, they've figured out that they can have a big influence on their children's education. You don't have to sit back and accept a second-rate education for your child. This book will give you pointers on how your school system works, so you can get involved.

Getting involved for the sake of your kids—that's what this book is about. That, and feeling good about raising your gifted child.

THE EIGHT GREAT GRIPES OF PARENTS WITH GIFTED KIDS

1. No one explains what having a "gifted child" is all about.

2. I don't like having my child labeled.

3. Relatives, other parents, and teachers don't recognize that we have unique problems. They assume it's a snap to raise a gifted child.

4. All parents like to think their kids are extra special. Some people think we're on an ego trip, or just plain pushy.

5. The school assumes that "the cream always rises to the top," so special programs for the gifted aren't needed. If that's true, then why is my child bored and unhappy with school?

6. Other people expect my child to be gifted in everything, or to act like an adult.

7. Parents get no support for this challenging job. Once you give birth, you're supposed to know it all.

8. It's exhausting to raise a gifted child! I wish there were ways to make it easier.

CHAPTER 1

Giftedness
Then and Now

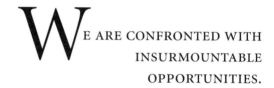

E ARE CONFRONTED WITH
INSURMOUNTABLE
OPPORTUNITIES.

POGO

Has giftedness always been valued?

Are gifted kids today getting the special education they need?

One of the first advocates for gifted children was Plato, Aristotle's teacher and founder of the first university around 380 B.C. He was all for testing and preparing children for Latin in early childhood. This was contrary to the popular belief of the time that giftedness was in the blood lines—a belief that has surfaced often since then, only now we call it the "nature vs. nurture" (or "heredity vs. environment") controversy.

In A.D. 800, the emperor Charlemagne urged the state to finance the education of promising children found among the common people.

A thousand years later, Thomas Jefferson believed that youth with potential should be provided with a university education at public expense.

By examining the history of education, we can gain insight and perspective into the role of gifted education in today's society. When society values knowledge, as in the Renaissance, talented people are recognized, appreciated, and educated. When society shuns knowledge, as in the Dark Ages, giftedness goes unrecognized and potential talent withers on the vine.

We can assume that there have always been gifted and talented people whose gifts have not been recognized, whose needs have not been met, and whose potential has been lost. The whole idea behind today's gifted programs is to make sure this doesn't happen in our time, with our children.

THE BIRTH OF THE WORD "GIFTED"

EDUCATION WAS NOT ORGANIZED in any systematic way until 1840-1850. Before then, only people with money (who could afford private tutors) or people with political connections (who were "favored" with learning) had the opportunity to be educated.

It wasn't until the early 1900s that the general public became interested in adapting education to those with more or less than average ability. At that time, the French government commissioned psychologist Alfred Binet, who had developed a test to measure people's "judgment" or "mental age," to screen out those children who weren't likely to benefit from a general education.

Binet's work was and is one of the most impressive contributions to educational psychology. Yet his articles and speeches would still be considered quite radical today. Binet believed that intelligence is *educable*— that it can be learned, expanded, and improved.

In 1916, American psychologist Lewis Terman took Binet's test to Stanford University in California and standardized it. Ironically, the Stanford-Binet Intelligence Scale assumes that intelligence is *fixed*—that it *can't* be learned, expanded, or improved. (Your child may have taken the current version of the Stanford-Binet at one time or another.)

Terman used the standardized test to identify gifted children in a study he was conducting. During the 1920s, he identified over 1,500 children with IQs of 140 or higher. In the general public, the average IQ is 100; Terman's subjects averaged 150. He followed these children from kindergarten through high school and into their thirties, publishing his results in 1925 and again in 1959.

Terman was the first to use the term "gifted," and his study was the most comprehensive long-term study of the gifted ever conducted. He published his findings in a five-volume work, *Genetic Studies of Genius*, that many people consider a classic.

MYTHS ABOUT GIFTEDNESS

TERMAN'S STUDY DISPELLED MANY MYTHS about giftedness, which until then had made it seem undesirable—a problem instead of a benefit. Today we still hear half-truths and fears about giftedness, remnants of those early myths.

One popular myth dates back to ancient times. For hundreds of years, researchers have tried to link genius with a "troubled mind." Italian sociologist and criminologist Cesare Lombroso sought out people who had gone insane or committed suicide and linked them to genius in his book, *Insanity of Genius,* published in 1895. Terman, however, found just the opposite. Gifted people, he asserted, are *more* stable than the general population. Any instability they may experience, he claimed, is the fault of their environment, not their giftedness.

More evidence for Terman's viewpoint has turned up lately. In recent years, psychologists have again been trying to find out whether very creative people suffer more often from certain psychiatric disorders. While a number of studies have found that a higher than average proportion of well-known poets, novelists, and artists have been victims of depression and other mood disorders, certain points stand out.

For instance, these very creative people tend to have only mild mood problems, not serious mental illness. Perhaps the simple fact of being an unusually creative person in our society—a society that doesn't always value such uniqueness—contributes to psychological problems. Peter Oswald, a San Francisco psychiatrist and author of *The Inner Voices of a Musical Genius* (about 19th-century composer Robert Schumann), believes there is a close relationship between the difficult lifestyle of talented and creative people and their anger, frustration, and depression. This makes a lot of sense.

Now let's back up a bit. Francis Galton, tying into his cousin Charles Darwin's Theory of Evolution, believed that intellectual ability was strictly biological. His book, *Hereditary Genius* (1869), held that heredity was the prime determinant of intellectual ability. Today we know that giftedness cannot be accurately predicted. Two genius parents may produce an average child, while parents of limited ability may have an offspring who is quite extraordinary.

Another myth about giftedness was the "Early Ripe, Early Rot" myth, which suggested that gifted people "burned out" at an early age. Some people thought that talent was quantitative—in other words, that you were born with a certain, specific amount, and once you used it up, it was gone for good. If you believed that, you certainly wouldn't want such a child. Nor would you dare to encourage early learning. Of course, Terman found that no such burn-out occurred. He even suggested that children can increase their abilities throughout their lives.

Terman also found that gifted people were highly productive, well-rounded, well-liked, and often chosen as leaders. He also debunked the myth that smart people are necessarily scrawny, bespectacled weaklings (as they are still so often portrayed). Instead, they are usually healthy and well-developed physically.

You should know that Terman's study has been criticized because he used predominantly Caucasian, middle-class, Jewish children, and he didn't take into account the influence of socioeconomics on personality differences. Further studies will have to be made before we can apply his conclusions to all (or even most) kids.

MODERN MISCONCEPTIONS

Misconceptions about gifted kids are still abundant today, which is probably why some parents are reluctant to have their children labeled "gifted." (Find out more about the pros and cons of labeling in Chapter 2.) These are some of the modern fallacies about what being "gifted" means:

★ The gifted don't know they're different unless someone tells them.

★ They'll make it on their own, without any special help.

★ They've got everything going for them.

★ They should be disciplined more severely than other kids because they should know better.

★ They need to be kept constantly busy and challenged or they'll get lazy.

★ They should be valued for their giftedness above all else.

★ They don't need to abide by the usual regulations, and they shouldn't be held to normal standards of politeness.

★ They should be equally mature academically, physically, socially, and emotionally.

THE NOT-SO-PRETTY TRUTH ABOUT GIFTED EDUCATION

GIFTED EDUCATION IN THE UNITED STATES has been the object of changing public opinion. On one hand, we as a nation believe in excellence, which means that everyone should be allowed and encouraged to reach his or her full potential. On the other hand, we believe that we're "all created equal," which means that singling out any group represents *un*equal treatment.

These ideas cannot coexist. As Thomas Jefferson so eloquently stated, "Nothing is more unequal than equal treatment of unequal people."

In 1941, Paul Witty of Northwestern University conducted a study for the U.S. Office of Education on programs for the gifted. His discoveries made dismal reading for anyone who cared about gifted education.

Witty found that only two to four percent of school districts nationwide had special services for gifted and talented children. When he singled out certain schools and school systems that did have gifted programs, he learned that those programs which had administrators who supported gifted services were frequently victims of their own success. That's because the good administrators tended to move on to further their own careers, and when they did, their districts often lost their gifted programs.

The American public got the sudden urge to "do something" when Sputnik was launched in 1957. Inspired by this 184-pound ball, we blamed our education system for its failure to keep up with the Soviets in math and science. Suddenly money for science education appeared and people in power started recognizing giftedness.

President Kennedy showed a commitment to reaching new heights (educationally and otherwise) when he promised to put a person on the moon. Now children were regarded as a natural resource, to be developed and used for the betterment of the country. As a nation, we searched out their potential, refined and packaged it, and sold that intelligence to the highest bidder—the most prestigious companies.

SEE-SAWING ATTITUDES

BY THE 1960s, PUBLIC RECOGNITION of the special needs of the gifted was again on the decline. Many people believed that using the IQ test to determine giftedness promoted elitism. Anything beyond the norm was regarded as suspect. In this era of protest, protesters everywhere sought to get rid of undemocratic "special treatment."

IS GIFTED ED ELITIST?

James Bray, writing in the May/June 1979 issue of *Gifted/Creative/Talented* (now *Gifted Child Today*), explains why it doesn't make sense to call gifted education "elitist":

"There should be a genuine effort on the part of those who work in gifted education to avoid a defensive attitude. Arguments of elitism are foolish. This nation fosters a sense of elitism when it comes to sports or the entertainment industry. Certainly there needs to be no apology for those who wish to nurture the minds of the best young students.

"No one needs to argue at the advent of the 21st century the need to solve problems in race relations, pollution, human rights, space exploration, health care or other vital areas. The problems are there, and the minds to solve the problems are there."

In 1964 the National Achievement Scholarship Program was begun to encourage black students. In awarding scholarships, the results of IQ tests were not given a high priority because they were thought to be biased against minorities.

There was renewed interest in giftedness in the 1970s, when one of the new buzzwords was "individualized education." Children who did *not* measure up were tested and diagnosed, their profiles were assembled, and educators wrote individual programs to match the diagnoses.

During this same decade, the Office of the Gifted in Washington, D.C. succeeded in setting up National State Leadership Institutes. The Institutes conducted research and resource conferences, and every state had a designated representative to develop a state plan for gifted education. Of course, not every plan was adopted.

THE MARLAND REPORT

IN 1970, A CONGRESSIONAL MANDATE required the Commissioner of Education to determine the extent of programs for gifted and talented students. With this information, educators could evaluate how existing federal programs could be used more effectively and what new programs could be recommended to meet shortages.

The commissioner's report, known as the Marland Report, stimulated interest not only in gifted and talented kids, but also in early education and treatment for the learning disabled and mentally deficient.

Here are some of the facts from the Marland Report the U.S. Office of Education presented in 1972:

1. Approximately 1.5 to 2.5 million children in the U.S. could be identified as gifted and talented.

2. Only 4 percent of these children were being served by special programs.

3. Ten states in the U.S. provided funding for special programs.

4. No state provided for all of its gifted. In those states that had special programs, at best only 50 percent of the gifted in those states were being served.

5. Only twelve universities in the country had graduate training programs to prepare teachers of gifted and talented students.

6. Of all schools surveyed for the report, more than half of the administrators reported that they had no gifted students within their district.

7. The overwhelming majority of gifted programs were at the high school level.

8. Research had established that school psychologists, more than other school personnel, were hostile toward gifted students.

9. Group IQ tests and teacher identification had failed to identify 50 percent of the gifted.

10. Available funding from federal sources for programs for the gifted was being used in less than 15 percent of the states.

11. Typically, half of the gifted students had taught themselves to read before starting school.

12. Approximately 3.4 percent of dropouts in a statewide survey were found to have an IQ of 120 or higher. Twice as many gifted girls as boys were dropouts.

And here's one last disturbing fact the Marland report divulged: The majority of the gifted child's school adjustment problems occurred between kindergarten and fourth grade. About half of gifted children became "mental dropouts" at around ten years of age.

PROGRESS, FINALLY

EDUCATION FOR GIFTED KIDS got its first real boost when legislative action awarded it $2.56 million in 1974. If the Marland Report was correct in its estimate of 2.6 million gifted students, that windfall amounted to...about one dollar per student. This figure has varied over the years, but it remains small in comparison to the budget for education of other children with special needs.

Giftedness was back in the public eye in the 1980s. This was the first time advocacy groups promoted giftedness in a grass roots movement. Today, almost every state has a coordinator for gifted education, even though federal money is always in short supply.

In 1985, the Richardson Foundation contacted 16,000 schools. The 10 percent that responded said they provided a variety of experiences for their gifted students, but nothing that added up to a substantial program.

The Richardson Foundation also found that gifted education was very fragmented. Even if a gifted class was available at one grade, there might be no gifted classes in the next grades up. Often, teachers taught what they were interested in, not necessarily what the students needed. Gifted education was regarded as an educational elective, for enrichment only, rather than something absolutely necessary—icing on the cake, rather than real substance.

In 1988, $8 million was appropriated for the first year of the "Jacob K. Javits Gifted and Talented Students Education Act." This was $1.75 million more than the highest appropriation under the 1981 act, and an excellent beginning towards an effective national program for the gifted. The National Association for Gifted Children, which moved to Washington, D.C. in 1990, has taken a leadership role in winning legislative battles and helping to ensure the success of this new national program.

Also in 1990, the Federal Department of Education awarded a $7.5 million grant to the University of Connecticut at Storrs to fund a new National Research Center on the Gifted and Talented. The new center's goal will be to develop new methods of identifying and instructing these kids.

Today, it seems, individual teachers are more aware of the importance of gifted education than in years past. As for the future, we can only hope that government budgets will someday provide school districts with the funds they need to help gifted and talented students fulfill their promise.

CHAPTER 2

What Makes Gifted Kids So Special?

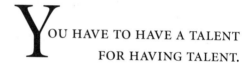

YOU HAVE TO HAVE A TALENT
FOR HAVING TALENT.

RUTH GORDON

What does "gifted" mean?

How can I tell if my child is gifted or talented?

How does my child's school decide who is gifted or talented?

Do some gifted kids "slip through the cracks" of the system?

One reason why it's so hard to decide who's gifted is because the word "gifted" means different things to different people. Here's a brief rundown of how some of the experts, past and present, have defined it:

▶ *Lewis Terman* defined gifted as "the top one percent level in general intelligence ability as measured by the Stanford-Binet Intelligence Scale or a comparable instrument."

▶ *Paul Witty* said, "There are children whose outstanding potentialities in art, in writing or in social leadership can be recognized largely by their performance. Hence, we have recommended that the definition of giftedness

15

be expanded and that we consider any child gifted, whose performance in a potentially valuable line of human activity, is consistently remarkable."

▶ *Dr. Joseph Renzulli* states that "giftedness consists of an interaction among three basic clusters of human traits—these clusters being above average general abilities, high levels of task commitment and high levels of creativity."

▶ *John C. Gowan* explains, "Gifted means having the potential to be verbally creative, while talented means having the potential to be non-verbally creative."

▶ *The U.S. Office of Education* declared in 1972, "Gifted and talented children are those identified by professionally qualified persons who by virtue of outstanding abilities are capable of high performance. These are children who require differentiated educational programs and/or services beyond those normally provided by the regular school program in order to realize areas of their contribution to self and society."

In its definition of giftedness, the U.S. Office of Education included these areas: general intellectual ability, specific academic aptitude, creative and productive thinking, leadership ability, visual performing arts, and psychomotor ability. (For some reason, psychomotor ability was dropped from their definition in 1979.)

▶ *Howard Gardner*, author of *Frames of Mind: The Theory of Multiple Intelligences*, believes there are seven human intelligences. Here's a quick inventory of the seven learning styles as applied to children:

- *Linguistic:* often thinks in words, likes to read and write, learns best by verbalizing or hearing and seeing words;
- *Musical:* likes to sing or hum along to music, appreciates music, may play a musical instrument, remembers song melodies;
- *Logical-Mathematical:* thinks conceptually, manipulates the environment in a controlled and orderly way, likes brain teasers, logical puzzles, strategy games, enjoys computers;
- *Spatial:* thinks in images and pictures, spends time drawing, designing things, using construction toys, is fascinated with machines;
- *Bodily-Kinesthetic:* has athletic abilities or dancing skills, may be good at typing, sewing, or carving;

- *Interpersonal:* understands people, is a leader, is good at mediating when his or her friends have conflicts.
- *Intrapersonal:* is deeply aware of his or her own feelings, dreams, and ideas, studies independently, may "march to the beat of a different drummer."

Typically, the two forms of intelligence schools deal with are those related to language and math. In these areas, special programs and kits are usually available for kids to follow. But for the other areas, there aren't any specific programs or materials, so it's pretty much hit-or-miss.

If a teacher is interested in music, he or she will make time for some units on music. If the school system doesn't have money, one of the first things to go is anything related to the arts. Hands-on, manipulative materials aren't heavily used, even though they're crucial to the development of spatial skills, because schools tend to be paper-and-pencil-oriented.

Interpersonal and intrapersonal learning are discouraged rather than encouraged. Kids are told to sit down and shut up rather than urged to communicate. We tell bright kids to be quiet and think a problem through, but we don't allow them to express their thinking skills verbally. If they do all their mental work in their heads, how can we catch their errors in thinking?

While there's a big move on now for "cooperative learning," this can be used or misused with gifted kids. It's misused when they end up being unpaid teachers. If they are consistently grouped with less able learners and are expected to carry the load for the group, resentment can build up on both sides. Besides, the gifted children aren't being stretched so they can reach their own potential.

THE CURVE AND THE LAW OF "AVERAGES"

THE BELL-SHAPED CURVE is one more way of approaching the idea of giftedness. To put it simply, if a test is administered to a lot of people, their scores will distribute themselves in a form similar to this curve.

Most people usually fall into the *average* range, which includes the large middle bump of the curve and a section on either side of the bump. Most school textbooks and curricula are aimed at this level, because that's where the bulk of the children are. If the whole population of our schools was given a test, 68 percent would score in that area.

Those who are *above average* are the next 14 percent up—those who do better on this test than the big group of people of average ability. The same goes for *below average*—that's the 14 percent below the big middle bump on the curve.

THE NORMAL PROBABILITY CURVE

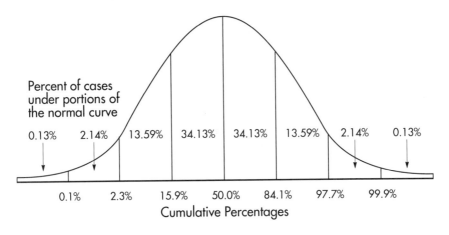

Percent of cases under portions of the normal curve

0.13% 2.14% 13.59% 34.13% 34.13% 13.59% 2.14% 0.13%

0.1% 2.3% 15.9% 50.0% 84.1% 97.7% 99.9%

Cumulative Percentages

When the average, above average, and below average are added together, that's 96 percent of the population. What's left? The *mentally disabled* are at the bottom, or far left. It's pretty well agreed that these youngsters need special help if they are to learn. The regular school curriculum won't work for them because they're too far from the average.

Last but not least, the most able 2 percent on the bell-shaped curve are called *gifted*. It's easy to see on the curve how the gifted are just as far from the middle as the mentally disabled.

The problem with this normal curve system is that the norm tends to become the ideal because it includes the most students. Those children who don't measure up to the norm get services and special educational treatment. And certainly that's good.

But what about the children who *exceed* the norm? The myth persists that they will do well no matter what, so their special needs are frequently neglected. We've found that gifted kids are more likely to adapt to whatever level we expect of them—usually the norm, or average—so they never reach their potential. Lewis Terman's successors have noted that exceptionally able students who were kept within their age groups instead of being placed with intellectual peers tended to develop lazy work habits.

HOW KIDS ARE IDENTIFIED AS GIFTED

IT'S TOUGH TO IDENTIFY each and every potentially gifted or talented student. But many schools today are trying. And most are using some kind of screening process to avoid judging kids ahead of time or arbitrarily assigning them to special programs.

In general, schools screen children using one or more of the methods described in this section.

Group Intelligence Tests

These are the well-known IQ tests, which have certain drawbacks. Although they're okay for initial screening, they may miss smart kids who have trouble reading, who have emotional or motivational problems, or who come from poor homes, especially those without much cultural enrichment. And the younger the child, the less accurate group test results tend to be.

Also, a child's IQ scores may vary from one test to another. Some districts use a cutoff point of 125 IQ to determine who gets into their gifted program, while others require an IQ of 145. Since there is so much more to any child than his or her IQ, as many as half of the potentially qualified children may miss being identified in this way.

Individual Intelligence Tests

These are more accurate than group tests when it comes to predicting intelligence, but they're costly and time-consuming to give. And even though they're more accurate at gauging IQ, this shouldn't be the only criterion for admitting any child to a gifted program. Besides, many experts say, these tests don't test intelligence; instead, they test academic aptitude within a specific culture.

Standard Achievement Tests

These tests measure achievement—"knowledge of or proficiency in something learned or taught"—rather than potential. Like group intelligence tests, they give results which school personnel should regard with caution. The "underachiever" may well be an unmotivated gifted child.

Sometimes it's a good idea to test bright children with older kids or those who are a grade or two ahead. These "off-level" tests give gifted young people a better chance to show what they know.

Teacher Nomination

When identifying kids for participation in gifted programs, some schools skip tests and rely on teachers' recommendations. But these recommendations aren't always reliable. Teachers have been known to identify those who achieve well, dress neatly, and do what's expected of them. It's easy for a busy teacher to overlook the highly creative, messy, unambitious, divergent thinker.

Still, teachers can provide valuable insights, *if they are trained* to look for the true characteristics of gifted and talented children, and not just for kids who are teacher-pleasers. These insights should be part of—*not* all of—the identification process.

Up to half of the qualified kids may be missed when the teacher's opinion is the only identifier. Researcher Jon Jacobs found that teachers at kindergarten level nominated gifted kids with only 4.3 percent accuracy.

One parent who felt sure that her second-grade son was gifted approached his teacher and asked to have him tested. The teacher said she'd do it, but she hadn't noticed anything unusual about the boy. "The only problem is that he reads his reading book when we're supposed to be doing math," the teacher said. Tests later confirmed that the boy was, in fact, gifted.

Parent Nomination

Here's where your expertise comes in. As a parent, you can provide wonderful insights into your child's abilities.

Researcher Jacobs found that parents of kindergartners were better identifiers of giftedness than teachers. The results of one study showed that parents correctly nominated gifted kids at a rate of 67 percent, whereas the rate for teachers (without training) was only 22 percent.

A DO-IT-YOURSELF INVENTORY

Here's an example of a checklist you can use to determine whether your child might be gifted or talented. (You might use the results to support your case with your child's teacher.)

A. What special talents or skills does your child have? Give examples of behavior illustrating these talents or skills.

_____

_____

_____

_____

_____

A Little	Some	A Great Deal	
☐	☐	☐	**B. Read each statement and decide if it describes your child a little, some, or a great deal.**
☐	☐	☐	1. Is alert beyond his or her years.
☐	☐	☐	2. Likes school.
☐	☐	☐	3. Has interests of older children or of adults in games and reading.
☐	☐	☐	4. Sticks to a project once it is started.
☐	☐	☐	5. Is observant.
☐	☐	☐	6. Has lots of ideas to share.
☐	☐	☐	7. Has many different ways of solving problems.
☐	☐	☐	8. Is aware of problems others often do not see.
☐	☐	☐	9. Uses unique and unusual ways of solving problems.
☐	☐	☐	10. Wants to know how and why.
☐	☐	☐	11. Likes to pretend.
☐	☐	☐	12. Other children call him or her to initiate play activities.
☐	☐	☐	13. Asks a lot of questions about a variety of subjects.
☐	☐	☐	14. Is not concerned with details.
☐	☐	☐	15. Enjoys and responds to beauty.
☐	☐	☐	16. Is able to plan and organize activities.
☐	☐	☐	17. Has above average coordination and ability in organized games.
☐	☐	☐	18. Often finds and corrects his or her own mistakes.
☐	☐	☐	19. Others seem to enjoy his or her company.
☐	☐	☐	20. Makes up stories and has ideas that are unique.
☐	☐	☐	21. Has a wide range of interests.
☐	☐	☐	22. Gets other children to do what he or she wants.
☐	☐	☐	23. Likes to play organized games and is good at them.
☐	☐	☐	24. Enjoys other people and seeks them out.
☐	☐	☐	25. Is able and willing to work with others.
☐	☐	☐	26. Sets high standards for himself or herself.
☐	☐	☐	27. Chooses difficult problems over simple ones.
☐	☐	☐	28. Is able to laugh at himself or herself.
☐	☐	☐	29. Likes to do many things and participates whole-heartedly.
☐	☐	☐	30. Likes to have his or her ideas known.

Creativity Tests

These relatively new tests show promise in identifying the divergent thinker—the child who comes up with many different responses to a problem—who may be overlooked on IQ tests. Creativity tests ask students to solve creative problems, with answers graded for *fluency* (the number of responses), *flexibility* (the ability to change one's mind set), *originality* (how unusual the responses are), and *elaboration* (the amount of detail included in the responses).

Here's a round-up of what the creative gifted child is like. (Some of these traits are described in more detail in Chapter 3.)

1. Is very curious about many things and constantly asks questions about anything and everything.

2. Comes up with a large number of ideas or solutions to problems and questions; often offers unusual, "way out," or clever responses.

3. Is uninhibited about expressing himself or herself and disagreeing with others, including adults; doesn't easily give up strongly held opinions.

4. Is a high risk-taker; may be adventurous and speculative.

5. Is intellectually playful; fantasizes, imagines ("I wonder what would happen if..."); fools around with ideas, changing and adding to them; likes to adapt and improve institutions and things.

6. Has a keen sense of humor and sees humor where others don't.

7. Is unusually aware of his or her impulses, shows emotional sensitivity, and is more open to the irrational in himself or herself. Boys may show a freer expression of "feminine" interests, while girls may possess a greater than usual amount of independence.

8. Is sensitive to beauty and notices the aesthetic side of things more than the average child.

9. Doesn't conform to the usual; is comfortable with disorder; doesn't mind being different.

10. Is good at giving helpful criticism and won't just accept what you or teachers say without examining these ideas or rules critically.

Products and Performance

When you're trying to decide if a child should be in a gifted program in the visual or performing arts, it makes sense to use actual physical evidence that he or she has unusual ability. When possible, an expert in the field should do the judging.

Top Percentile of Honor Roll

If you identify gifted kids only by their grades, this may favor achievement-oriented teacher-pleasers. A student's position on the honor roll also depends on which classroom he or she happens to end up in, and can vary greatly from building to building and from district to district. Besides, some hard-working students will always manage to get excellent grades without being unusually intelligent or able.

Pupil Motivation

Task commitment—or stick-to-it-iveness—often leads to great accomplishments. Dr. Joseph Renzulli, relying on Terman's studies of the gifted, states: "The four traits on which the most and least successful groups differed most widely were persistence in the accomplishment of ends, integration toward goals, self-confidence and freedom from inferiority feelings. In the total picture, the greatest contrast was in all-around emotional and social adjustment and in drive to achieve." The problem arises when you try to *measure* motivation.

Peer Nomination

Students themselves often have a fairly good idea of who the gifted kids are in their class, but you can't just run a popularity contest. These days, testers are using cartoons with younger children to locate those students who are known by their peers for their cleverness, leadership ability, or ingenuity. In one test, the test-giver shows a child a picture and asks, "Who would Moppet ask for help when he is lost? Or when he's in need of a special invention?"

WHAT HAPPENS NEXT?

IF ANYTHING YOU'VE JUST READ makes you suspect that your child is gifted or talented, the next move is yours. Talk to your child's teacher, and, if necessary, discuss your observations with the principal.

Start keeping records of your child's progress and achievements so you can back up your claims. You may even want to keep a notebook with examples of your child's work, books read, and pictures of projects. In some cases, the gifted child's ability is evident, especially in the performing arts or athletics. In other cases, special gifts or talents are less obvious and harder to see.

In some instances, school personnel may be the first to spot a child's talents, but *you usually know your own child best.* In fact, if a teacher is *not* trained to identify giftedness, the bright, creative child may appear to be more of a pain than a pleasure in the classroom. If your child fits this picture, you may need to speak with the school counselor, psychologist, administrator, or curriculum specialist. (For tips on getting your school to improve its gifted programming, see Chapter 6.)

THE QUESTION OF LABELS

SOME PARENTS, as well as a number of experts, question the use of the "gifted" label. But labels already exist, and yes, they create expectations. When you question children, they already know quite accurately who's in which ability group. Teachers may assign neutral names to such groups—for example, "Bluebird" for the top readers, "Robin" for the average readers, "Sparrow" for the slower readers—but kids are very aware of what these labels really mean.

The controversy over "tracking"—putting kids in ability-based groups—is valid. Many educators have a real concern for kids who are labeled and never given a chance to rise above that label. For the gifted child, tracking is a mixed blessing. Once you label a child as gifted, you've

created a problem that didn't exist before. Now you find yourself asking if you're doing everything you possibly can to stimulate this child. It feels like a bigger responsibility than you had before.

For the gifted child, knowing that she's in the "fast" or "high" track may only reinforce something she already knew about herself. Acknowledging giftedness doesn't necessarily give a kid a big head, which some people are afraid of.

But if a gifted child is misdiagnosed and placed in a lower track, it can be deadly. Sometimes kids are placed in tracks not because of their overall ability, but because of their ethnic background or their linguistic ability or difficulty. Or the child who's very verbal may be identified as gifted when he's just super talkative rather than genuinely brilliant.

HOW KIDS FEEL
ABOUT THE "GIFTED" LABEL

★ *"I don't mind being called gifted as long as I'm not stereotyped as being perfect."*

★ *"I feel comfortable with the label if I'm in a group of people who are considered gifted—then I want to be considered gifted, too. But I'd certainly never introduce myself as a 'gifted person.' I'd never seek out that label, but I'd always want people to say, 'Yeah, she's a bright student, she's an inquisitive student, she's going to go far.' I think the label has positive and negative connotations."*

★ *"I do not like being called gifted; it's embarrassing and it's like bragging."*

★ *"I don't know of any other word to replace 'gifted' but I wish someone would think of something."*

Labels *can* cause problems if you're not careful. According to recent research conducted by Dewey G. Cornell, Ph.D., a clinical psychologist and professor at the University of Virginia, it's better for parents *not* to emphasize the gifted label. Cornell found that those children whose parents openly refer to them as gifted have less favorable self-images, are more prone to anxiety, stress, and depression, are less well-liked by their peer groups, and have more behavior problems.

According to Cornell, these difficulties are due to parents focusing too much on this one aspect of their children's personalities and having too many expectations. When parents do this, kids are likely to think their self-worth depends only on being gifted.

Cornell's sensible advice is to downplay the label and encourage your kids to be well-rounded, kind, and friendly. In his study, the children of parents who did this had fewer problems than the others.

HOW PARENTS FEEL ABOUT THE "GIFTED" LABEL

Some parents favor the use of "gifted," while others would gladly eliminate it. Here are some of their comments:

Mother of an eighth grader:

"I'm not certain that the 'gifted' label is in the kids' best interests, nor in the parents' interest. To me it fosters inflated egos and sometimes elitist attitudes, and may increase the pressure to excel to justify their giftedness."

Mother of sixth and eighth graders:

"Those who don't have a child in the program have a problem with the label. I don't."

Parent of first and third graders:

"For my child, who's very hard on herself, thinking she's gifted makes her feel better about herself. However, it's embarrassing at times."

Father of third and eighth graders:

"I think it causes resentment from their peers. There must be a better term to use."

Mother of a ninth grader:

"There's more of a chance the teacher will be interested in the children and able to develop challenging activities."

KIDS WHO FALL BETWEEN THE CRACKS

CERTAIN GROUPS OF CHILDREN have a way of "falling between the cracks" of the system, so their teachers miss the signs of individual giftedness or talent. If your child fits one of the categories described in this section, her abilities may not show up on standardized tests. Or her giftedness may not be obvious. As a parent, you'll need to pay especially close attention to see that your child's needs are met in the classroom. When gifted kids don't get the attention they need, they tend to underachieve, disrupt the class, and even fail.

Start recording some of the activities your child has been involved in, and what she was aiming at by doing them. (If you don't know, ask her.) Is she pursuing a special interest? Do her abilities surprise you? Present this information to the gifted program coordinator or to your child's teacher or principal.

Young Boys with a Lot of Energy

When high energy mixes with low tolerance for frustration and pressure, this can signal trouble. Many times little boys are very tactile learners who don't sit still and do the paper and pencil tasks teachers

require. That can make it difficult to identify their intelligence, and even tougher for teachers to meet their needs. Sometimes boys are thought to have an attention deficit disorder, while out of the school setting their giftedness may show up better.

Teenage Girls

Females in our society are not necessarily rewarded for being smart and good in school. Unfortunately, not only does sex-role stereotyping still exist, but it becomes increasingly evident in the middle and high school years. It's not "cool" to get an A when the guy you want to date is struggling with his schoolwork.

Parents can help girls feel more comfortable about using their gifts by showing an appreciation for their abilities. *The Colorado Handbook for Parents of Gifted Children* suggests that parents try these tactics—the sooner, the better:

▶ Encourage your daughter to seek companionship with people who value her abilities, rather than those who are threatened by them.

▶ Help her find male teachers who are supportive of her when she does things that aren't typical of girls.

▶ Point out and introduce her to intelligent and professional women in many fields as role models.

▶ Hold high expectations for your daughter (without being unrealistic—this causes problems, too).

▶ Avoid sex-typed toys and books.

▶ Avoid being overprotective. Let her climb trees and move about the neighborhood freely, if she wants to.

▶ Encourage high levels of activity. If you notice her watching boys playing actively, encourage her to join in.

▶ Allow her to fail.

▶ Repeatedly tell her that you believe in her abilities.

▶ Support her interests, whatever they are.

▶ Find other gifted and talented kids—peers she can identify with.

▶ Foster an interest in math and science, and never discourage her from pursuing a career in traditionally male fields.

▶ Assign chores on a non-sexist basis (brother and sister should both take turns doing the dishes and washing the car).

▶ Discuss sexist stereotypes on TV, in movies, and in rock videos.

▶ Encourage her to spend time with her father or another male relative— an uncle, cousin, grandfather—doing something they both enjoy doing, even if it's a traditionally "masculine" activity.

Kids with Disabilities

Disabled or not, Thomas Edison, Albert Einstein, Ludwig van Beethoven, Helen Keller, and Franklin D. Roosevelt all possessed special gifts. Consider Mrs. Einstein. She didn't give up on her son, even when his school did, and eventually taught him to read through non-conventional methods. Like her, you can become an advocate for your child.

Look for the following problems, which could be getting in the way of identifying your child as gifted or talented:

▶ difficulty with memorizing, learning math facts, spelling, reading, timed achievement tests, or remembering instructions with more than two steps;

▶ a wide gap between subtest scores (great in verbal, awful in math), or gaps in scores between different tests (high today, low tomorrow), or a profound difference between behavior at home and at school;

▶ poor motor coordination;

▶ repeated ear infections, especially within the first three years, since these can cause problems with a child's hearing, and learning problems may develop as a result;

▶ difficulty completing easy work, but ease with harder concepts;

▶ poor self-concept; a feeling of being stupid;

▶ allergies.

Wayne, a young boy, always became lethargic around the same time each year. He would perform poorly in school and his test grades would drop dramatically. His mother took him to an allergist and found that her son was allergic to a particular pollen that was released into the air during the time of year Wayne was having problems. The appropriate medication allowed him to function much better.

Gifted disabled children need to be identified and helped early. This often calls for specially designed tests that compare them with other disabled kids. Armed with the results of these tests, the school should work together with the parents and other resource personnel to come up with programming that makes sense for these kids.

Children from Minority Cultures or Bilingual Backgrounds

These children may be overlooked because their home culture or language is different from what the teachers are used to. Though they might well be gifted or talented, they don't *appear* to measure up to the standards of the majority culture. Of course, their self-esteem suffers when this happens.

If you're a minority or bilingual family, make it a point to get to know the school staff. Let them know about your family. Tell them about any special activities your family is involved in, and keep them informed of your child's achievements or accomplishments outside of school.

Sarah, a young girl from a Spanish-speaking family, had a high IQ, but since English was her second language, her teacher didn't have any idea how bright she was. Her family was very involved with church activities. By the time Sarah was in second grade, she had memorized many Bible verses and performed a big part in a church play. Her teacher didn't know anything about these activities until Sarah's mother brought them to her attention.

Teachers need to put aside the question of verbal skills, at least for the time being, when they're looking at someone from a home where English is not the main language. You can identify giftedness no matter what language students speak if they:

▶ act independently,

▶ know how to get their ideas across, including non-verbally,

▶ show leadership and initiative,

▶ are imaginative,

▶ are flexible when approaching problems,

▶ show signs of being able to think abstractly,

❱ learn quickly,

❱ remember and use information and ideas well, and/or

❱ are unusually curious.

Young Children

Because tests don't accurately measure what young children know, this special population is often overlooked. The problem is further complicated by the fact that specialists in gifted education are not usually specialists in early childhood education, and vice versa. Plus few states provide funding for programs designed for young gifted children.

Still, the sooner gifted kids are identified and given appropriate challenges, the better their chances for reaching their full potential.

Poor Children

If you're poor enough, you're probably too busy struggling for survival every day to worry much about whether your kids are gifted. Even if you've noticed their unusualness, the effort it takes to get them into a good gifted program may seem overwhelming. Here's where a sharp teacher can save the day. Many successful adults whose families were poor can point to teachers in their past who made a difference—recognizing their abilities, offering special encouragement and opportunities.

PUTTING THINGS IN PERSPECTIVE

IN OUR RUSH TO IDENTIFY gifted kids, and our determination to make sure that no one gets overlooked or mislabeled, we're bound to make mistakes. It helps to remember that definitions of gifted and talented change with time and vary by culture. Once, accurate hunting ability must have been the most highly prized talent; today, hunting is primarily a sport, and some people consider it barbaric. Fire-bringers, fortune-tellers, athletes, and entertainers have all been esteemed in certain periods and cultures but not in others.

If today we place a premium on IQ and creativity, what might we value tomorrow?

● ● ● ● ● ● ● ● ● ●

READ MORE ABOUT IT

To find out more about the ideas in this chapter, read:

Frames of Mind: The Theory of Multiple Intelligences by Howard Gardner (Basic Books, 1983). An intelligent discussion of the different ways people think and excel.

Growing Up Gifted by Barbara Clark (Charles E. Merrill, 3rd edition, revised 1988). A detailed, textbook-like guide to all aspects of giftedness and gifted education. Dr. Clark's book is one of the most thorough available on the gifted, and is used in many college classes.

In Their Own Way: Discovering and Encouraging Your Child's Personal Learning Style by Thomas Armstrong, Ph.D. (Jeremy P. Tarcher, 1987). A clearly written guide aimed at parents and teachers.

● ● ● ● ● ● ● ● ● ●

CHAPTER 3

Living with
Your Gifted Child

G ENIUS IS AN INFINITE CAPACITY
FOR GIVING PAINS.

DON HEROLD

What are gifted and talented kids like?

What day-to-day adjusting should I do
as a supportive parent?

Your gifted child is a unique individual who shares certain characteristics with other gifted children. You've probably noticed by now that your
child learns differently, acts differently, and reacts differently from your
friends' children of more average abilities. You can no doubt think of
instances when your youngster has done something especially charming,
precocious, or embarrassing. It's likely that you've been impressed or
surprised by some unexpected behavior.

This chapter looks at the characteristics most bright youngsters share.
With this knowledge, you'll be able to do the best possible job of meeting
your own child's special needs.

ENDLESS QUESTIONS

GIFTED KIDS ARE THIRSTY for knowledge. Some of them want to know all about everything, and others want to know everything about one thing at a time.

Their questions are endless. From the minute they wake up until they collapse, their minds are at work trying to make sense of their world. Even at lights-out, their questions continue. You'll notice this even when they're very young. More than one parent has put it this way: "My child is like a sponge, trying to soak up everything."

KIDS ASK THE DARNEDEST THINGS!

"Why is the moon a different shape tonight than it was last Tuesday?"

"How do people know what 'pretty' is?"

"How do helicopters go straight up?"

"What did Grandma wish when she blew out the birthday candles when she was a little kid?"

"How do wars start?"

"Why don't frogs have fur?"

"How does water stay together?"

As you know by now, some of your child's questions *can* be answered (even if not by you), while some don't have definite answers. It's always a relief when a child asks something that can be looked up—except, of course, when the answer is beyond a young child's comprehension. A smart child can ask more questions than a wise parent can answer.

What can you do to prepare for the barrage of whys, whens, what fors, whos, and how comes? Start early to accumulate a good set of assorted reference books—a current almanac, an atlas, a book of world records, a book of facts, a dictionary, a one-volume encyclopedia, perhaps even a whole set of encyclopedias. You'll want to help satisfy that curiosity as soon as possible, whenever possible, and you can't always get to the library on the spur of the moment.

As for the tougher questions, be honest. Depending on your child's age, you might say something like, "That's a really good question. A lot of adults have asked that question, too. The problem is, we don't have a great answer to it. What do *you* think?....Well, here's what *I* think."

ACTIVE FOR A REASON

GIFTED KIDS (AND THEIR PARENTS) soon find out that learning and discovering are intense processes that require constant activity. Some children are so active, in fact, that they're wrongly considered hyperactive. One important difference is that gifted kids often appear driven to explore their world. They use their seemingly endless energy to achieve a goal: getting to know the world better. The hyperactive child, in contrast, tends to be active without a particular goal or purpose.

Because their minds are as active as their bodies, many bright kids may actually spend less time sleeping than other children. They need as much sleep as anyone else; it's just that they have a hard time settling down. They may be the first in their age group to give up naps. Plan for lots of active, imaginative, outdoor play to make use of some of that energy.

Relaxing bedtime stories serve a real purpose besides sheer enjoyment—they help kids' minds gear down, as well as their bodies.

REMEMBER WHEN?

GIFTED AND TALENTED KIDS generally have excellent memories, which they frequently put to good use by reminding their parents of things they may have forgotten (or wished to forget). One mother reported that she got a speeding ticket when her son was three years old and he *still* remembers it—time, place, and speed—at age nine.

These children recall years later who gave them what at holiday time, and what promises were made and not kept. Do comments like these sound familiar?

▶ "Two weeks ago last Tuesday you promised we'd go for an ice cream cone and we never did. How come?"

▶ "When I was four, you said you'd build me a tree house soon. Well, I'm ten now, so...."

Obviously, you'll keep your child's trust a lot longer if you don't make promises you aren't sure you can keep.

EARLY WALKERS, SPEEDY TALKERS

YOUNG GIFTED KIDS MAY WALK AND TALK earlier than their peers, although there are exceptions. A few very bright, perceptive youngsters may prefer to wait to talk until they can communicate in complete sentences, or they may wait to walk until they can do so without falling. These children usually will observe others first, then progress at their own pace.

One four-year-old watched carefully as his six-year-old brother repeatedly fell while struggling to learn how to ride a two-wheeled bike. One day the four-year-old simply got on the bike and rode without falling. As the years went on, he learned many other physical tasks the same way, by watching and learning from others' mistakes (most frequently his brother's, to his brother's dismay).

If your child is like most gifted kids, she probably possesses a "motor mouth" that rarely shuts down. These kids also tend to have sophisticated vocabularies that alienate them from their peers, who simply don't understand the big words. For example, the young gifted child may want to discuss dinosaurs with her playmates, but rather than talk in general terms, she'll get specific about Brontosaurus, Stegosaurus, and Tyrannosaurus Rex.

Bright children not only hear and understand big words; they can also apply them in the correct context. One three-year-old was fooling around to delay his bedtime. When his mother asked what he was doing, the verbally precocious youngster replied, "I'm procrastinating!"

ACROSS THE AGES

GIFTED KIDS MAY BE ONE AGE EMOTIONALLY, another age physically, and still another age intellectually. Your child may have one set of friends who are age peers and another set of friends who are intellectual equals.

Bright children definitely need others like them to play with and share ideas. You'll notice that when there are only a few such youngsters in a larger group, they tend to find each other.

When the other children your child's age are not at his mental level, he may claim someone much older as his best friend. It's common for a very smart five-year-old to choose a nine-year-old down the street to hang around with, explaining, "He's got good ideas." This turns into a problem when your child's older friend wants to go to the park and your five-year-old isn't allowed to cross the busy street yet. The nine-year-old may also take off on a two-wheeled bike and leave your little one behind.

New situations and problems are bound to come up when your child hits the teen years. His intellectual peers are dating, driving, maybe drinking, but he's neither emotionally nor legally ready for those milestones.

The talented child who has skipped a grade somewhere along the way may suffer most intensely from this discrepancy. Gifted kids often feel "different" to begin with, and adolescence intensifies this feeling, while the desire to be accepted causes even more pressure. Above all, your child needs to feel that *you* love and understand him.

What are the two most difficult periods of a gifted child's childhood?

1. The preschool years, when the child doesn't know what's wrong but somehow knows he's "different." He may even wrongly see himself as "dumb."

2. The teen years, because peer pressure is *so* important. When teens feel the pressure to be like everyone else, they sometimes *under*achieve.

Sometimes problems arise at home because of the gap between intellectual and emotional ages. You may say to your child, "Act your age," when that's exactly what he's doing. Silliness is a prime example. You might scold your child for acting silly, even if you would tolerate the same behavior in a less-gifted child.

Some adults, even though they believe that "kids will be kids," feel that gifted kids should "know better." A five-year-old may be able to read at a fourth grade level or solve amazing math problems, but he's still only five years old. Accidents may happen, thumb-sucking may persist, shoelaces may go untied, and babyish behavior may surface from time to time.

Never punish your child because he's acting "childish," or because he's gifted and "should know better." Try to relax and let him be a kid for as long as he needs to be. Take the word of many parents who have gone before you: Your silly child will be grown up and out of your hair before you're ready.

Don't you wish, just a little, that you had time for more silliness in your busy life?

THE MOTOR SKILLS GAP

YOUR YOUNG CHILD'S MANUAL DEXTERITY is probably not advanced beyond her years, and she may actually lag behind her age mates in this one area. This can be frustrating, since her understanding and knowledge go far beyond her ability to do something with her hands.

A bright child's handwriting may not be as good as either she or her teachers would like it to be. Gifted kids often find the act of writing slow, tiresome, and discouraging, especially since their minds usually work far faster than their pencils. Consider letting your child dictate her ideas into a tape recorder when she's fed up with writing. If you've got a computer, teach your child to use it as early as possible. Computers can be very freeing, especially for creative work, since they eliminate most of the tedium from correcting errors.

Help your young child develop her small muscles by playing with playdough, finger paints, or stringing beads or cereal. She probably dislikes restrictive, prescribed ways of doing things, so permit her extra freedom to express herself with art materials. Teach handwriting as an art form—calligraphy. This makes it fun and challenging to form letters, rather than sheer torture. Physical activity of all kinds helps youngsters become well-rounded in their motor skills.

COPING WITH YOUNG LAWYERS

HAVE YOU EVER FOUND that a person three feet high could out-argue your best efforts at logic? If your gifted child is like most, he learned early to use his excellent verbal ability to get exactly what he wants. But just because he's good at it, don't let him dictate the rules and regulations of the house. Children feel more secure if their parents set a few important rules and stick to them, no matter what. Giftedness is no excuse for disobedience or obnoxious behavior.

When you deal too strictly with most children, they have a tendency to get angry and act aggressively toward other children. This goes for the bright child, too. Only he may take this further, and may also learn to lie or steal at an early age if he senses a need to. So it's especially important that you treat your child with fairness and respect.

Giftedness doesn't mean moral superiority, however. That is, your child doesn't deserve more lenient rules just because he's smart. But he may learn more quickly than the average child which consequences to expect from what sort of behavior—so he doesn't have to make the same mistakes repeatedly. Maybe.

Bright children need to understand the structure of the world so they can function within it. If gifted kids continually manage to outsmart their parents and teachers and gain control, as they attempt to do at times, they may end up feeling lost and confused. Even youngsters who have superior knowledge appreciate the security of knowing that someone wiser and more experienced is in charge.

As your child matures and you see him making sound decisions, you'll be able to trust him more and more. If he argues with you because he truly believes truth and justice are on his side, at least listen carefully to what he has to say. There's no shame in being won over by the superior arguments of a young lawyer, as long as he's not arguing for the sake of arguing, and as long as you don't go against what you deeply believe.

Wear-down, break-down situations simply aren't healthy. With practice, you can tell when your child is arguing just for the sake of pushing limits, and when he really has rational principles on his side. If he can base his arguments on having proved his responsibility in some area, maybe it's time to loosen the rules and broaden his freedom.

THE COMPANY OF ADULTS

YOUR CHILD MAY BE MORE COMFORTABLE with you and other adults than with other children. This kind of dependency happens for a couple of reasons. Gifted kids often feel the frustration and limitations of their age, and they may, in fact, interact better with adults than with their peers. They may truly enjoy adult conversations and prefer adult company.

They also can figure things out quite well, but don't have the ability or skills necessary to carry out what they understand intellectually. So they feel that they need adults to help them fulfill their goals.

A five-year-old once asked me to write a letter to the editor of our local newspaper. He was deeply concerned about an injustice, and he knew that those in authority wouldn't listen to a five-year-old but might consider his solution if it were presented by a teacher. I sat down with him and he dictated his ideas to me. I submitted his letter under his name. He was satisfied that his ideas were presented, and I was satisfied that I was assisting him while using his words.

Helping is fine, but don't get caught in the trap of talking for your gifted child—as in, "Dad, I want *you* to tell my teacher that I can't _____." The bright child, who recognizes that a teacher will more readily listen to a parent's ideas and requests, figures, "Why not get mom or dad to do the talking?" It's important that your child knows you support her, but she also needs to learn to speak for herself.

THE IMPORTANCE OF RISK-TAKING

SOME OF US ARE GLAD that our kids aren't more daring than they are, at least when it comes to physical thrills and spills. But when it's a matter of taking a chance on a new activity, or sticking one's neck out to meet an intellectual challenge, it's sad to see some gifted kids hold back from running even the slightest risk. These mostly younger or insecure children want to know what something is all about, how it will work, and what's involved *before* making a commitment.

Some bright kids won't venture out until they've observed others in similar situations. They *hate* to be wrong, to look foolish, or to not know what's happening. Now, watching others is a fine way to learn something— within reason. But if your child's caution is prompted by a strong fear of failure, you'll want to help him feel better about himself. He needs to know that not being able to do something right the first time is *not* the same as "failing," and that even repeated "failures" don't make him an inadequate person.

Be sure not to fall into the trap of making killer statements like, "That's ridiculous!" or "That could never work!" Such statements discourage your child from using his imagination—which is the last thing you want to do. Show that you value your child's work, along with the sometimes uneven process he went through to complete it. You can encourage positive self-esteem with comments like, "I can see you really put forth a lot of effort on that." Risk-taking requires an atmosphere of acceptance. Give your child permission with, "Try it and see what happens."

One way to help your youngster abandon the assumption that all questions must have a "right" answer is to pose problems that don't. Try these: "How would you improve the family car?" "What would you do if you won the lottery?" "How is a statue like a sunset?"

WHAT'S SO FUNNY?

WITH THEIR ADVANCED UNDERSTANDING of the world, gifted children often have a mature sense of humor. They catch the punch lines in jokes—both those they hear and those they make up—when other children may miss the humor completely. Because of this, your child may become frustrated because other kids don't get the joke. Some bright youngsters prefer adult company partly for this reason.

Smart kids often get a special kick out of puns and plays on words. If you can keep your own sense of humor at times like these, you'll avoid many a disaster. One parent reported that her son appreciated and understood adult jokes from about age four.

Just be warned: If thwarted, the gifted child's keen sense of humor can turn to biting sarcasm. If you see this habit forming, point out that children who always put others down, even jokingly, are usually unpopular.

GIFTED WORDPLAY

★ While the teacher was discussing temperature in class one day, the thermometer fell over. Five-year-old Evan remarked, "We'd better get our coats because the temperature dropped."

★ Five-year-old Tran said to her father, who was leaning over a bowl of spaghetti, "Watch out! If your tie falls in the plate, you'll have Thai food."

★ "What's a cat's favorite food?" is a riddle that recently made the rounds at one primary school. The answer: "mice crispies." And what do polar bears like to eat? Try "ice crispies."

FAST LEARNERS, DEEP LEARNERS

ALMOST ALL GIFTED KIDS learn basic skills better and faster than other children, so they need less practice and repetition to master new tasks. If they are made to go over and over the same stuff they already know, they get bored and lose their motivation. Even kids who are tops in math, for example, make careless errors when they tire of doing the same type of problem repeatedly.

Gifted and talented children often have many interests, but they usually like to concentrate on one specific area at a time. They become "specialists" at an early age as they gather and retain an amazing amount of information about their chosen area.

Take heart, parents: Kids *do* pass from one all-consuming passion to another. But next year could be worse! If you thought dinosaurs were bad...*living* reptiles could follow. One mother finally had to make a rule: Nothing alive, and nothing that had ever *been* alive, could be brought into the house without her permission. Her daughter had been bringing home "road kill" to dissect so she could study animals' insides.

Most bright children enjoy working on projects, preferably ones they have chosen for themselves. They like to discover knowledge by figuring things out for themselves. At times, they may take on more than they can handle. For example, one fifth-grade boy decided that he would do a school project on "wars." Obviously, the topic was too broad. When the teacher asked what specifically interested him, he replied, "Weapons," and further narrowed this to weapons of the Civil War. Now he was able to focus his energies for an excellent paper.

Help your child to be realistic when it comes to attacking projects. Often a youngster will do part of the planned work—just enough to satisfy her need for information—and then quit. After all, research can be the most fascinating part of a project, while the write-up feels anticlimactic. If a finished product is truly needed—say, for an important school project—you may need to lend a guiding hand. Otherwise, be prepared to accept unfinished projects and frequent shifts in direction. Discuss the change of interest, then let your child move on without guilt.

FEARS AND WORRIES

GIFTED AND TALENTED FOLKS of all ages tend to be acutely aware of problems. It's common for them to develop fears and anger about war, starvation, poverty, abuse, violence, and all the other injustices in the world. In other words, they worry about Big Stuff!

Researchers Jeffrey Derevensky and Elaine Coleman investigated the fears of gifted kids and compared them with those of children of normal intelligence. Among younger gifted children, the most common feared category included some form of violence and nuclear war. This emphasis on violence may reflect what kids are reading and hearing about in the news media—reports of kidnappings, molestations, murders, and other terrible acts.

Bright children also were found to have a diverse variety of miscellaneous fears, emphasizing their increased awareness of the world. Some of their concerns included death and disease; fear of getting pregnant, and of having an abortion; unemployment; lack of friends; loneliness; bankruptcy; being abandoned; lack of love; and mental disorders. In this study, the fears of an eight-year-old gifted child compared with the fears exhibited by a non-gifted ten year old. One young gifted girl feared that she or her mother would end up schizophrenic, just as her aunt had been diagnosed.

A recent study by Richard R. Klene of the University of Cincinnati sought to determine the best way for parents to help their gifted children get over their fears. Discussing the fearful situation or reassuring the child about it were the least effective methods parents use, though they are used most frequently. What *does* work is setting a good example, and gradually exposing the child to the feared thing.

Gifted kids are so perceptive that even at a young age they realize the inevitability of death. They question the meaning of death, and some even become obsessed with dying. They may act out dying or bring home dead animals to bury.

While death is a natural process, coping with the death of a family member may not be. Few of us in this death-denying culture feel comfortable talking to children about death, but children can end up feeling guilty and somehow responsible when everyone's feelings are kept hidden. Their questions need to be answered frankly and truthfully, or else the unspoken message is that death is so bad that it shouldn't be faced.

If someone your child knows dies, recall the happy times you all shared with the deceased, and let the child know it's all right to cry when we're sad. Use puppets, art materials, and perhaps a journal to help your child work through her sad feelings. Bibliotherapy—reading books on the topic of death, dying, loss, and grieving—can also be helpful. Answer as many of her questions as you can, and if possible, include her in the funeral process to help bring closure.

Whether young children should attend the wake and view the body is a matter of considerable controversy. Some professionals think it's a good idea; others strongly disagree. You may want to consult your family doctor, your minister or rabbi, or the school counselor if you feel you need help making this decision.

SOUND MINDS IN SOUND BODIES

NEVER MINIMIZE YOUR BRIGHT CHILD'S NEED for lots of physical activity. At times, his body is (and should be) as active as his mind. Moving to music, learning to ride a bike, running, and walking are just a few of the obvious choices. Help your child use his imagination to come up with creative ways to get physical.

Here are a few stimulating physical activities to try:

▶ Creatively change games to bring new excitement to old favorites. For instance, when playing ping-pong, the person who wins the first game plays the next game with her "wrong" hand (left hand if she's a righty).

▶ Play "All on One Side." This is a volleyball game with four or five players on one side, none on the other, and a balloon for a ball. Each player volleys the balloon to another player, then scoots under the net. The last player to touch the balloon taps it over the net and scoots under. The receiving players try to keep the balloon in play and repeat the process. The object is to get your team to the other side of the net and back as many times as possible.

▶ Walking is a terrific, life-long exercise. Take different kinds of walks together with your child. For example, try a "never-before-seen" walk. As you travel a familiar route, look for ten things (or fifty) you've never noticed before.

CONCENTRATION AND RELAXATION

GIFTED KIDS OFTEN HAVE a long concentration span for things that interest them. Your youngster may be so totally preoccupied with a book, bug, or project that she won't hear you say it's time for a meal. She's not ignoring you; she's just absorbed and unaware.

One parent reported that she had trouble getting her child's attention when he was reading. Eye contact works wonders, especially after you've given a gentle touch or hug. Yelling is useless. It merely develops children who become "parent deaf."

You'll reduce everyone's frustration if you let your child in on plans and scheduling ahead of time. You probably wouldn't like it if someone told you, "Put that book down right now! We have to go to the store." You'd prefer to hear, "I need to go to the store at 3 o'clock. I'll let you know ten minutes before we have to leave." If your child is the kind who becomes very engrossed in and stimulated by a project, you may have to help her learn to "come down."

Physical exercise can be very relaxing, but some children get such a high from it that it becomes another habit. One boy I know became so accustomed to that high, excited feeling that he was almost using it as a drug. For him, exercise was no longer a form of relaxation but another activity he felt driven to do. If you notice your child becoming over-involved in any activity, step in and help her strike a balance in her life. Encourage her to try new things, to play, to be with friends, and even to take time off just to be lazy.

Gifted children are particularly sensitive to the sights, sounds, and other stimuli of their environment. They may be deeply affected by nature, music, or colors. They notice small nuances in their world that others may be blind to. At times, your child may feel bombarded with sensory infor-mation—as if everything is converging on her. She'll need to get away, either by relaxing where she is, or by physically escaping to a quieter place. Can you think of a room or a corner in your home where your child can go for some privacy and peace?

Some bright children have a hard time getting to sleep. They can't leave a stimulating book or TV show and go straight to bed without some-thing in between. They need "unwind time." Or sometimes they'll go to sleep with no trouble, then wake up in the middle of the night with their heads full of wonderful ideas. A tape recorder beside the bed can give them a way to record their thoughts and release them so they can get back to sleep.

RELAXATION TECHNIQUES FOR TALENTED KIDS

★ Teach your child to meditate, as you understand meditation. For example, you might suggest that he clear his mind, focus entirely within himself, ignore any external distractions, and play calmly with any thoughts that enter his mind.

★ Counting breaths serves a dual purpose: it's relaxing, and it helps to control a wandering mind. Have your child count each breath, one by one, up to 10, then start over again. He can repeat this process as often as necessary to feel calm and refreshed. Explain that if his mind wanders at any time during this exercise, he should go back to 1 and start counting again.

★ One way for your child to relax physically is by tensing his entire body all at once, then relaxing it all at once, letting every part of his body go limp.

★ Another way is to begin with one body part (perhaps the fingers of one hand) and let it go limp. Proceed to consciously relax every part of the body one by one, from the ears down to the toes.

WHEN NEATNESS DOESN'T COUNT

IT WON'T SURPRISE YOU to learn that bright children aren't always neat. In fact, they tend to have a special tolerance for confusion and junk. We're talking about kids who may solve tomorrow's energy crisis but can't find a pencil today because it's buried under open books, half-completed projects, LEGO cities, stamp collections, and other evidence of their many and varied interests.

Neat assignment papers are probably not a priority, and a neat room—by your standards—is almost always out of the question. Gifted kids in general hate to throw things away. They can tell you exactly when and where they found the valuable rock that's on the dresser, and which bird lost the feather that's under the bed. They're so acutely observant and aware of details that they're sure to notice if something is missing. Moral: Respect their belongings, and don't expect to get away with simply tossing what *you're* tired of.

Schools don't teach time- and clutter-management skills, so you'll need to come to the rescue with a bit of organizational savvy. For example, you might hold a weekly "what-do-I-want-to-keep?" session. Although your child may prefer to hold on to all those papers she brings home from school, have her sort through them, choose those which have special value to her, date them, and put them in a special place.

A variety of different storage boxes can work wonders. I had my children label folders by the month and file them in a big box. Then, at the end of the school year, I had them sort through them. I asked them to consider, "What do I want to remember about this year?" Boxes can also be used to classify important "junk" or pieces of precious art work. When the boxes are full, then it's time to sort, reorganize, and decide what to toss—or get more boxes.

Allow your child her own "space," usually her bedroom, which will undoubtedly be less tidy than you'd like. But you may certainly set a *few* house rules, such as: Everything has to be up off the floor on Saturday mornings (or whenever the vacuuming is done); no food litter allowed in the bedroom; and all personal belongings are to be removed from common areas, such as the living room, daily (or weekly, if you can stand it).

EARLY READERS

SOME GIFTED KIDS are self-taught readers. With most of these young children, we don't know when and how they cracked the code. Early reading, however, isn't always a sure sign of giftedness.

Some children are taught to read by parents or preschools as early as age three. Others may have other interests, and to them reading isn't a priority. In fact, the bright child who doesn't read by the end of kindergarten or first grade shouldn't be eliminated from (or passed over for) a gifted program. Similarly, the preschool child who reads shouldn't be admitted to a gifted program on that criterion alone.

In a study reported in 1980 in *Gifted Children Newsletter*, researchers Jack Cassidy and Carol Vukelich challenged the assumption that superior intelligence is demonstrated by advanced early reading skills. Among the 58 children they observed in a special program for gifted pre-kindergartners, only about 20 percent of four- and five-year-olds were reading. The mean IQ of this group was 158. The mean IQ of the 80 percent who were not yet readers was only three points lower.

Gifted children master reading, like so many other tasks, when they're ready *and* when they see the benefits it can bring them. They seem to "crack the code" without letting us in on how they do it.

THE IMPORTANCE OF STAYING IN TOUCH

MOST BRIGHT KIDS are cooperative, sociable, and well-liked. They're often regarded as leaders. Parents need to make sure that these talents are channeled in a positive direction. Many gang leaders are kids whose talents have been negatively channeled.

Make it a point to know what your child does after school, in the evenings, and on the weekends. Know who his friends are. Get to know his friends' parents, too. Call and introduce yourself; you may find that they feel the same way you do and are pleased to hear from you. If you're dropping your child off at another child's home, don't just drive away. Walk up to the door and meet the parents.

Even though most kids want their parents to be less openly involved in their lives as the years go by, you can still stay in touch if you do it diplomatically. Whenever my kids are going to a party, I always call to make sure that one or both parents will be home the entire time. I also confirm that no alcohol or other drugs will be available.

Peer group influence can put tremendous pressure on any child. One family I know had a gifted daughter who had always been a super student and a super kid. When she started high school, her behavior deteriorated and she became withdrawn. Her parents eventually learned that she was using drugs. The girl explained that she felt that she didn't "fit in" with any of the kids in school. So she found a group outside of school who did accept her. Because they were using drugs, she did, too.

I tell my teenagers that our home is always open. I'm willing to spring for the pizza, the soda, and the chips, and I'll rent the videos. That way I get to know the kids my kids are hanging around with, and I maintain some degree of control over what they do together.

● ● ● ● ● ● ● ● ● ●

READ MORE ABOUT IT

To find out more about the ideas in this chapter, read:

The Centering Book: Awareness Activities for Children and Adults to Relax the Body & Mind by Gay Hendricks and Russell Wills and *The Second Centering Book: More Awareness Activities for Children and Adults to Relax the Body & Mind* by Gay Hendricks and Thomas B. Roberts (both Prentice Hall, 1989).

Growing Up Creative: Nurturing a Lifetime of Creativity by Teresa M. Amabile, Ph.D. (Crown, 1989). What to do and what to avoid so your child is free to be creative.

The Joys and Challenges of Raising a Gifted Child by Susan K. Golant (Prentice Hall, 1991). A first-person account of life with a gifted daughter.

Parents' Guide to Raising a Gifted Child: Recognizing and Developing Your Child's Potential by James Alvino and the editors of *Gifted Children Monthly* (Little, Brown, 1985). A practical volume covering schoolwork, critical thinking, creativity, the arts, problems, etc. Alvino has also written *Parents' Guide to Raising a Gifted Toddler.*

Playing Smart: A Parent's Guide to Enriching, Offbeat Learning Activities for Ages 4-14 by Susan K. Perry (Free Spirit Publishing, 1990). A compendium of creative activities requiring little preparation.

● ● ● ● ● ● ● ● ● ●

CHAPTER 4

Coping with Problems

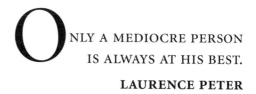

O NLY A MEDIOCRE PERSON
IS ALWAYS AT HIS BEST.

LAURENCE PETER

How can I keep my child from being labeled a "nerd"?

How can I cope with my child's super-sensitivity?

How do I deal with perfectionism?

When does normal gifted behavior cross
over into the danger zone?

When and how should I get help?

Let's say it right out: Gifted and talented kids are difficult to parent.
Right now, you're probably thinking, "That's the understatement of the year!"

Your child is likely to be more extreme, persevering, and intense than
the average child. As a result, you can expect to encounter some problems.
This chapter highlights some of the more typical ones, along with a few less
common but more serious challenges to be on guard against.

HOW NOT TO RAISE A NERD

MOST OF THE TIME, gifted kids get along well in the social arena. But their independence of thought and nonconforming behavior may give them (and you) some uncomfortable moments. These traits occasionally appear abrasive to others, both children and adults.

What is a "nerd," anyway? It's just one of many names people call others who are different from themselves. Legions of youngsters who haven't figured out the current formula for ultimate "coolness" have been stuck with this insulting label. Sometimes they actually bring it on themselves, and wouldn't be considered so nerdy if they only had a few more social skills.

Here's where you come in. Point out, gently, what it takes to be accepted by other kids. Discuss with your child the attributes of the more popular kids. Not that you'll want him to emulate all of these traits and behaviors—just the more positive ones. Find out what *he* thinks they have that he doesn't.

Some children choose nerdiness as a way of coping. They do certain irritating things in an effort to boost their self-esteem. If, for example, they believe they *always* have to know the answer and *always* have to be right, their peers are bound to find this abrasive. Many gifted kids feel that they can't ever let themselves be wrong. They feel that to compliment someone else, or to acknowledge that a classmate had a good idea, somehow diminishes them. So they tend to be stingy about complimenting others. They have trouble sharing the limelight. This doesn't make for much popularity among the playground set.

Sometimes bright children are labeled nerds just because their interests differ from those of their age peers. Unfortunately, no matter how hard they try, some of these kids are always going to have a tough time fitting into certain social groups. For them, the trick is to find groups they *can* fit into, or to settle for one or two really good friends—probably other smart youngsters—who understand and accept them.

Gifted children frequently suffer from feelings of isolation. This can be especially painful during their teen years, when peer approval is so important. Teens want desperately to be like everyone else, from their haircuts to their tennis shoes to the labels on their jeans. With some bright kids, this happens as early as third or fourth grade, rather than the more usual middle-school years. The child who thinks differently can feel alienated at any age.

If the gifted teen feels like a failure socially, he may give up and focus only on his mental abilities. Although he shouldn't be pushed into social situations which aren't comfortable for him, everyone's life needs some balance, so you may want to encourage your child to at least keep an open mind about making friends. Even socially adjusted gifted kids may have fewer social contacts than some other teens, since they may limit their inter-actions to a range of people with similar interests and abilities.

One way you can help is by bringing to your child's attention books about other successful nonconformists. When a bright young person reads biographies, he can see that people of eminence have had to work hard and struggle in order to overcome big problems. That can make his own life seem more manageable.

Suggest that your child find a pen-pal and join special clubs, such as a chess club or Mensa (a national organization for people with high IQs). Your state gifted coordinator might be able to point you toward other possibilities, including parents like you with kids like yours.

The key to real "social adjustment" is how a person feels about him-self. Self-esteem begins at home and develops best in an emotionally healthy family. Gifted classes are another way for your child to form positive self-esteem.

FLASH!
GIFTED CLASSES BOOST SELF-ESTEEM!

Read what other parents have said about their children's experience with gifted classes:

Father of a high schooler:

"Being in a gifted program changed my son's behavior so that he seems more at ease with himself, enjoys school more, and isn't teased by his classmates for being bright. He's also more challenged by class work."

Mother of a fourth grader:

"Last year, after enjoying academics for the first three years of school, my daughter began to lose interest. She faked illnesses and getting her to school was a fight. This year, now that she's in a gifted program, she's out the door early and home with a burst of news each day."

Father of a sixth grader:

"My son is less disruptive at school. His self-esteem increased as a result of his participation in gifted classes."

Mother of a ninth grader:

"The gifted program has helped my daughter with tremendous self-confidence and an overwhelming desire to hear and be heard. The program enriched her already existing talents."

Father of a seventh grader:

"My son put it this way: 'It would be hell to go to a school without a gifted program!'"

DEALING WITH SENSITIVITY

GIFTED KIDS TEND TO BE SENSITIVE, and some are even *super*-sensitive. Their heightened awareness makes them especially vulnerable. For example, if an entire class is scolded, the bright child may wrongly assume more than her share of the blame. This is the child who feels devastated when someone dislikes her. Try to get across to your super-sensitive child that she's going to encounter people who simply don't like her, for whatever reason, just because of her particular personality (even though *you* think it's terrific).

The gifted child knows who her true friends are. If someone tries to use her, butter her up, or get on her good side, she senses the falseness behind those actions. When she hears, "You're the best at doing this, and I would like to have you do it," she knows she's being manipulated. She can tell if someone tries to fool her, and she hates being the butt of a joke.

Gifted kids are also alert to small changes in their environment. They notice everything. At the same time, they're super-aware of their own interests and intellectual abilities. Paradoxically, this may diminish their self-esteem. This is because many bright kids focus on how they're *different* from their peers rather than how they're *similar*. They forget that they're human beings, just like their peers, and feel set apart in a negative way. They perceive their differences as weaknesses rather than strengths.

This is especially true for highly creative children. The artist's perception is not necessarily like anyone else's. I know an excellent portrait artist who, when he looks at other people, notices if their eyes are too close together, if their chin is unusually long, if their nose is disproportionate to the rest of their face, if their eyebrows are too full, and so on. He told me that whenever he tried to explain his perceptions, people would say, "My, but you're critical!" To him, his observations aren't critical at all; they're just his way of seeing. However, he *did* notice a change in his social life when he started being more tactful.

Since gifted children are so sensitive to their surroundings, they end up with more "stuff" to process. Newspapers, TV newscasts, and adult conversations all contain things to worry about which youngsters can't always process correctly. Parents may not even be aware that a child has heard this information, let alone that the child is anxious or afraid because of it.

For example, many of us today are concerned about the environment and whether we're going to have enough oxygen to breathe in the future. Many sensitive gifted and talented kids have appointed themselves "ecology police" in their own homes, where they point out with great seriousness that their parents aren't recycling or purchasing the "right" products. Many a parent has been put on the spot by a child who asks, "Mom, how come you're still using styrofoam cups?" (Not that we all can't learn something from our kids, if we're willing to listen.)

Gifted young people are also able to read non-verbal language and may wrongly interpret behavior. They may think, "Mom and Dad had an argument about me, so if they get a divorce it will be my fault." These children need to be encouraged to verbalize and share their feelings and concerns *before* they become overwhelmed by them.

One five-year-old grew extremely worried when his grandmother was working on her income tax. It turned out that he was concerned because she had mentioned her IRA. On the TV news the night before, he had heard that the IRA was responsible for a bombing in Ireland. He thought this meant that his grandmother might somehow become the victim of a bombing!

Gifted kids' passion for justice and truth makes deceit and insensitivity unbearable to them. It's not unusual for them to take on the cause of the underdog. Their super-sensitivity also makes them super-aware of hypocrisy and social injustice. They often turn away from self-concern earlier than their age peers, and get interested in reforming the world. One ten-year-old girl likes to make a wish on the first star she sees each night. But she never wishes for toys and clothes for herself. Rather, she wishes for peace on earth. She has also recognized and is able to discuss the fact that over-population is a serious world problem.

These children tend to be idealistic and insist on answers to uncomfortable questions. They see atrocities on the news. They read about unfairness and unethical practices in the newspaper. They fail to understand how we, their parents, can allow all this to go on.

HARD QUESTIONS

It's not unusual for gifted kids to ask hard questions like these:

★ "Why do people have to go hungry?"

★ "Why are shopping centers built on prime farm land?"

★ "How come industries continue to pollute?"

★ "How can we end terrorism?"

★ "How can politicians say one thing, get elected, and then do something else?"

★ "Why are there wars?"

★ "Why do we supply weapons to countries so that defenseless people are killed?"

Someday soon (if it hasn't already happened), your child may question your religious beliefs. She may want to explore alternative beliefs. And she may not accept "Because I said so" as a reason why she should act or believe in a certain way. For example, if your family goes to church together every week, she may decide that she no longer wants to go. She needs and deserves to be heard. And she needs and deserves to hear honest answers in return, even if the best you can do is, "We've been members of our church for years. Worshiping is something we do together as a family. You're part of our family, and it's important to us that you be there, too. You can make your own decisions about church when you're older."

Gifted children may see the world as a scary, ugly place to grow up into. For this reason, they may act particularly immature at times. Being babyish is safe. To act like an adult and think like an adult may seem like too much of a burden. One of your goals is to encourage your child to develop her capabilities, to help her feel empowered, and to show her that she can use her mind to help solve problems. She needs to learn that hoping problems will go away or pretending they don't exist won't get her very far. Meanwhile, try to take some comfort in your child's idealism—it's the hope of the future.

INTOLERANCE AND THE TOO-SMART MOUTH

IT HAS BEEN SAID that gifted children "don't suffer fools gladly," and some of their parents do little better. But even bright kids must learn that there are times when being right isn't important. Good manners and common politeness may sometimes mean holding your tongue. For example, when Grandpa uses incorrect grammar, as he has his entire life, it's probably better to accept the words in loving fashion, rather than to criticize him.

Some gifted youngsters who are rejected by their peers don't have a clue about how to solve the problem. You need to teach your child tactfulness and the other social amenities, no matter how high his IQ may be. Teach him the routines of everyday politeness, such as how to write thank-you notes. Tell him that he mustn't say, "Wow, you're a fat lady," because "The lady might take that as a hurtful thing to say, and she will hurt inside, just as you would hurt if I said something bad about you." Make it clear that there are times and places for questions to be asked and answered that won't offend others.

If your child seems to have an especially large and critical "mouth," it may mean that he doesn't feel particularly good about himself. By cutting others down and pointing out everyone else's faults, he may be trying to raise his own self-esteem. He may be saying to you, "Look at *me* and notice how good *I* am." Just because *you* know your child is gifted doesn't necessarily mean that *he* knows or believes he is. Even when people repeatedly tell them how smart they are, many gifted young people fear that they'll be "found out" as not-so-bright after all.

TOO GOOD: THE PERFECTIONISM PREDICAMENT

ONE OF THE MOST COMMON, most destructive problems many gifted kids face is *perfectionism*. They drive themselves (and others around them) crazy trying to achieve some ideal version of "success." If your child acts as though failure is incredibly awful, and the only way to get attention is to be perfect, you've got a serious dilemma to deal with.

What's so bad about perfectionism? To begin with, since its victims think they have to be perfect, they don't like to try out new experiences. So they end up limiting their own options, just to be sure nothing can happen that might reveal their flaws. Trying means maybe failing—judged by their own impossibly high standards—so these kids never achieve a fraction of what they might.

Perfectionism even explains some cases of underachieving. When there's a huge gap between the ideal and what the child sees herself as being capable of, sometimes she simply gives up. Then she can always say she didn't try. A number of bright kids go so far as to drop out of school.

Gifted and talented children need to be taught that learning, by its very nature, means taking risks. Real learning is not always achieved on the first attempt. Sometimes it takes practice, trial-and-error, and doing over again. The hardest idea to get across is that missing a goal doesn't equal failure; instead, it can be an opportunity to grow. That's why it's so important to allow these kids to experience failure within a safe environment. Don't set your child up for failure, but *do* provide experiences in which she'll have to stretch herself.

Be careful to do this in a nurturing, encouraging way, not in a stress-filled, ego-damaging way. Well-run gifted classes can provide these types of opportunities. After her third-grade daughter entered a gifted class, one mother said, "She's no longer bored with school! She's had to learn to work to achieve good grades. She also believes there's nothing she can't learn if she just tries!"

You can do a lot to keep your child from suffering the pangs of perfectionism. When you focus on the negative, or talk constantly about how important it is to "make the grade," "grow up," "get ahead," or "do better," you're putting pressure on her. Some kids respond by dawdling on the easy tasks to avoid harder ones. In fact, some perfectionist gifted kids work so slowly that it drives teachers and parents to distraction.

Others may procrastinate by postponing work, again hoping to avoid failure. Let your child know that you understand her desire to do well and recognize her fear of goofing up. Then work at making your home emotionally safe for exploring new topics and ideas.

The gifted child may rip up paper after paper because her writing or drawing doesn't look like the example in the book. Coloring books tend to discourage children's creativity because the prescribed form is right there in front of them. It's preferable to allow your child to experience the real object and draw her own impressions. Show her master artists' concepts of different subjects so she can observe for herself how varied creative expression can be. The more you let her know that you value uniqueness and originality, the more free she'll feel in her own efforts.

If you're in awe of your child's amazing abilities, you may unknowingly be contributing to a pattern of non-stop reaching for more and higher and better. How? By praising every milestone, every action, every day. Sure, praise can be positive, but not if it's constant. Sometimes this can bring about an unhealthy response.

For example, if you praise your child for every accomplishment, does the absence of your praise on a particular occasion mean that you don't appreciate what she's just done? Not necessarily, but she might believe this is the case. Suppose you're in the habit of saying, "Honey, you look nice today." Seems innocent enough, doesn't it? But if you say it every day except one, simply because you forget to say it that day, your child is likely to assume that there's something wrong with the way she looks.

Because bright kids do most things well, it's easy to fall into the pattern of praising without thinking. Your child could end up feeling pressured to keep doing well, and fearful that she won't be able to over the long term. People who are praised too much sometimes believe that they're valued for their accomplishments, not for themselves.

Does this mean that you should stop praising your child? Of course not. Just concentrate your good words on your child's *efforts*. Say, "It looks like you're really excited about this report," or "Isn't it fun that you get to learn so many neat new things while working on this project?"

Whatever you do, don't go in the opposite direction. Criticism is a sure killer of initiative, creativity, and imagination. Resist the temptation to say "I told you so" or "You should have known better." It's much more helpful to say, "What can be learned from this?" (As long as you don't say it in a "holier-than-thou" way that disguises "I-told-you-so" feelings.)

Some children rarely forget an ill-timed criticism. I know I'll never forget this one: In the first grade, we were supposed to draw a picture of a red barn. I made mine pink because I wanted it to look weathered, as though it had been out in all the elements. I can remember the teacher saying that my barn wasn't as good as the other kids', and not putting it up on the board because it was pink. But there was a logical explanation!

PUT-DOWNS VS. POSITIVES

How do you talk to your child? When it's time to point out a problem or a fault, are your words constructive or destructive? Encouraging or discouraging? Here are some common parental put-downs—and positives to try instead.

Instead of this:	*Try saying this:*
"What happened here?"	"How do you feel about your report card?"
"Why can't you ever do it right?"	"You do a good job of...."
"You still can't do...."	"You have really improved in...."
"Why don't you ever...."	"I like it when you...."
"Go look it up."	"Let's find out together."
"That was a dumb thing to do!"	"So you made a mistake. What did you learn from it?"
"Act your age."	"I understand how you feel."
"Are you still working on that?"	"Keep trying. Don't give up."

Be aware that your child may show extreme concern about her appearance. Even young gifted kids may get unreasonably upset when their hair won't behave. They want the image they project to be as perfect as can be, for they believe if they look perfect, they may become perfect.

Some bright children show their perfectionism by becoming extremely anxious before tests. Perhaps they think that if they fail, others will discover that they don't know as much as they've been given credit for. They fear that they will be looked upon as "impostors." To them, even an A-minus is a failure.

One way to help your child avoid the perfectionist trap is to make sure that the tasks she is given (at home and at school) are neither too hard nor too easy. If she's given tasks that are too easy, she'll form poor work habits and assume that everything will always come easily to her. Some gifted kids have breezed through high school but flunked out of college for this very reason. On the other hand, if your child is given tasks that are too difficult or not clearly defined, she may simply give up. Like most young people, gifted children do best when an assigned task is a little *above* their ability level. Given *slight* frustration, they have to reach. And that's how they grow.

Sometimes the best thing you can do for a budding perfectionist is *listen*. Offer a calm comment when you see your child suffering frustration. Say "You'd like that to be finished perfectly," or "You're really struggling. I appreciate your effort." Remind your child kindly that *everyone* fails on occasion—that it's okay. Keep your eyes peeled for biographies of top achievers. They'll help prove to your child that struggle and even failure often come before great accomplishment.

For example, Thomas Edison tried 1,500 different filaments for the light bulb before finding the right one. After the last experiment, an assistant asked, "Well, Mr. Edison, how do you feel about having 1,500 failures to your credit?" Edison replied, "No, they weren't failures. We now know 1,500 light bulb filaments that don't work!"

Even if you and your child's teachers aren't applying overt pressure, your gifted youngster may still be plagued by internal stress and strain. Some perfectionist kids develop ulcers, tics, or nervous disorders if they don't find suitable outlets or release valves for their tension. Exercise, relaxation techniques, good eating habits, fun, and laughter all help.

The perfectionist has a low tolerance for mistakes. Instead of being proud of completing a task or running a race, the bright child may only notice that she didn't win any prizes or break any records. Set realistic goals for yourself, and help your kids do the same. Learn to relax yourself. Model acceptance of your own mistakes, showing that you're not crippled for life by a dumb error.

Help your child distinguish between times when it's important to give your all, and times when it's best to just let go. Some tasks are not worth doing well—they're routine jobs that just need to be done. For me, dusting is one of these tasks. Another is washing the car. No one ever inspects my car to make sure every speck of dirt is removed. There is no "Clean Car Award," yet it's important to remove the road dirt, and road salt in snowy winter weather, on a regular basis. In the whole scheme of things, other matters take priority in my life. Similarly, I teach my children to set priorities in their lives.

Most important, try to model non-perfectionist behavior yourself. If you don't have time to clean the house before company arrives, it may be momentarily upsetting, but it's not a life-threatening crisis. If you make a mistake at home or at work, talk about it and let it be known that it's not the end of the world. Disappointments and failures, large and small, are a natural part of life.

WHEN TO WORRY

HOW CAN YOU TELL when one of your child's problems has gotten out of hand and it's time to call in the cavalry? Occasionally it's well worth the effort to seek out a school psychologist, therapist, or some other professional who has seen and dealt with similar situations before. But the dividing line isn't always obvious between "It's just a passing phase" and "Uh-oh, this has gone too far and has been going on too long."

Be open to the suggestions of school personnel. Be ready to hear both positive and negative things about your child without trying to rationalize or defend his behavior. School officials often complain that too many parents deny that a problem exists when it plainly does.

Ten Tip-Offs to Trouble

How can you tell when something beyond the regular and routine is happening in your child's life—something that may cause real problems, now or later?

Here are some danger signs to watch for. Don't ignore them! When you deal with difficulties early, they don't become unmanageable. And if it turns out that you were worried over nothing, allow yourself a sigh of relief.

1. Self-imposed isolation. Start to worry when your child spends all of his time avoiding you, the rest of the family, and every kind of social situation, even ones involving friends he used to like.

It's normal for young people to lock themselves in their rooms for lengthy periods, but it's usually to talk on the phone with their buddies. If your child seems to spend most or all of his time alone, consider this a warning sign.

2. Extreme perfectionism. If the only tasks your child enjoys are those he can do perfectly, and if he's not willing to take a single risk or try anything new, then this is a degree of perfectionism you can't ignore. Also be alert to the child who gives up easily and won't try anything at all because he lives in terror of failure. Either way, he's probably miserable and could use some help.

3. Deep concern with personal powerlessness. We all need to feel that we can have *some* influence on the world and what happens to us. The gifted child who feels utterly powerless is convinced that he can have no affect on adult situations or world events. He may strike back by developing a negative attitude or an undercurrent of anger, or by name-calling or putting others down. He may begin distrusting adults and "the system."

4. Unusual fascination with violence. TV and movies aren't the only culprits, but these ever-present media do expose children to violence and brutality beyond their comprehension. Some become immune to it. Others become fascinated by it.

Don, a bright boy who learned by doing, was such a case. His parents were used to his constant questions and experiments. Yet they noticed a definite change some time after he began bringing home dead animals to dissect. At first, he was led by pure scientific curiosity. Gradually his interest took a bizarre twist, and he began mutilating and torturing animals. Cruelty to animals is a red warning flag.

5. Eating disorders. In our society, thin is generally considered beautiful. It's not hard to understand why girls in particular may become obsessed with being very slender. When they fear that a single additional ounce will make them less attractive, they may go so far as to nearly starve themselves to death. This disorder is called *anorexia nervosa*. Even if the dieting girl is actually quite slender, in her mind's eye she sees FAT.

Take Ann. Her slender older sister is a cheerleader, homecoming queen candidate, and all-around good student. Ann wishes she could be more like her thin, beautiful sister. Although Ann is a good student, too, she doesn't view herself positively. She wants to be more perfect, more like her sister. Looking at herself in the mirror, she sees herself as fat, although at 14 she's a trim 95 pounds. So she decides to diet. "If I don't eat, I won't gain weight," she tells herself. But soon, not gaining weight isn't enough— she wants to *lose* weight. She's sure that if she does, others will like her more. The pounds don't come off soon enough for her, and her parents become upset with her for not eating. They insist that she eat, and so she does, only to go into the bathroom and throw up afterwards. She may even binge eat and then regurgitate, which is typical of **bulimics.**

Two studies reported in the *Journal of the American Academy of Child and Adolescent Psychiatry* indicate that gifted girls may be more prone toward eating disorders such as anorexia and bulimia. Both studies found that the girls' self-concept was the most important factor. Those with symptoms of eating disorders tended to have problems with low self-esteem, hypersensitivity to the opinions of others, loneliness, and confusion about their feelings. Those who lacked support systems at home and school were especially vulnerable. The characteristics of being highly self-critical and hard on themselves that gifted kids exhibit are found in most anorexics, although in an extreme form.

Uncontrolled eating is another type of eating disorder. This person is comforted by food, the more the better. "Pigging out" can also be a socially acceptable form of rebellion. Like the anorexic, the overeater sees her world as out of control. Eating is one area that she feels she *can* control. (Nine out of ten of those who suffer from eating disorders are female.)

6. Substance abuse. Gifted kids are subjected to many pressures: to be accepted, to excel, to change the world. When the pressure becomes too great, it's natural to seek a release. Healthy releases include exercise, meditation, relaxation techniques, and so on. Unhealthy releases include the abuse of alcohol and other drugs.

Jerry was a good student, well-liked and talented in gymnastics. He worked hard to perfect his skills, spending all of his free time in the gym practicing routines. All was well until Jerry began junior high at a new, large school where he had few friends. Cliques formed and Jerry felt left out. A few kids urged him to try smoking. This appealed to him, since it made him feel important, even though it went against his training.

Gradually Jerry's new friends urged him to try some stronger stuff that would get him high. He wanted so badly to be accepted that he agreed to try what they offered him. The high he achieved resembled the high he worked so hard to get in gymnastics, only it came so easily. He became accustomed to this easy high, until eventually his parents noticed that something was wrong. Jerry's grades dropped drastically. He withdrew from family activities, preferring to spend long periods of time alone in his room. Then his parents discovered that he was skipping classes. They finally realized that Jerry was using drugs and sought outside help for him.

7. Preoccupation with self. Narcissism has existed through the ages. With the media and ads promoting physical beauty as the sure route to acceptance, love, and happiness, some youngsters overdo their concern about their appearance.

Of course kids should care about how they look, and plenty of youngsters spend hours in front of the mirror. However, if you suspect that your child is taking this too far, check with other parents. How much time do their kids spend primping in front of the mirror and worrying about their clothing? Start considering it a problem when the behavior interferes with normal functioning, or your child seems to be thinking *only* of himself.

8. Withdrawal into a fantasy world. When the real world feels too dangerous or threatening, the gifted child may withdraw into his own make-believe world.

Consider Alan. When he was an infant, his parents divorced and his mom left. He lived with his dad and fraternal grandparents. In preschool, he astounded teachers with his exceptional ability. Already he could read, tell time, and do advanced math computations. When his mother returned to town, she and his father fought over his custody. Alan was all too aware of the turmoil. He couldn't deal with the tension, so he withdrew into an imaginary world with imaginary friends. At least he could talk with these friends without fear of disapproval. His contacts with the real world became less and less frequent.

9. Rigid, compulsive behavior. Some gifted kids refuse to do anything but study. This compulsive behavior pattern often starts because they're having serious difficulties finding anyone they can relate to intellectually. Since highly gifted students think differently from most other kids in their neighborhood or school, and they sometimes lack social skills, they may have a hard time making friends. So they choose to withdraw to their books.

When Jill was a young child, it was obvious that she was very bright. When she didn't get her way, she threw temper tantrums and cried easily. Because she was bossy and controlling, she was never able to develop friendships that lasted longer than a few days. In the classroom, she was the "know-it-all" who had a habit of tossing out trivia and useless information. Teachers and peers shunned her, and she was taunted on the playground. For comfort, she turned to her books, which became her only real friends. Counseling helped rescue Jill from this limiting behavior.

Another kind of rigid, compulsive behavior is almost the opposite of Jill's. Some gifted and talented children are super-achievers—over-scheduled kids who are busy, busy, busy. Parents may not catch on that something's amiss with these youngsters, because they seem to be able to do everything and keep it all in balance. They get top grades, excel at sports, run their own small businesses, and still find time to win the lead in the school play! The trouble is, they may burn out early.

Excessive fatigue is a tell-tale sign that all is not well. If you've got a Superkid, you may need to limit the number or kinds of activities she participates in, for her own good.

10. Preoccupation with death. *Never* ignore this warning sign! The statistics about the rise in teen suicides and attempted suicides are shocking and tragic. It's estimated that 6,000 teens per year end their own lives, and ten times as many try. These numbers could be on the low side, since many families don't talk about it when their kids try to kill themselves.

People with above-average intelligence may be more prone to suicidal ideas and characteristics than others. Why? Perhaps it's because they have such high expectations of themselves and others, they're often perfectionists who perceive failure everywhere (which contributes to a feeling of powerlessness), and their relationships are often unusually intense.

If your child exhibits any of these signs of a teen in trouble, get help quickly:

- sudden changes in personality, behavior, eating, or sleeping habits;

- alcohol or other drug abuse;

- lack of interest in planned activities, withdrawal from family or friends, self-imposed isolation;

- severe depression that lasts a week or longer;

- concealed or direct suicide threats;

- talking about suicide, either jokingly or seriously;

- preoccupation with death and death-related themes;

- giving away prized possessions;

- feelings that life is meaningless.

HOW TO GET HELP

AT SOME POINT in your child's school career, she may benefit from a few sessions with a school counselor. Studies have found that gifted kids may need more than the usual amount of guidance to achieve and maintain good mental health. A competent counselor can help your child understand and value those differences that set her apart from her peers.

Don't wait until there's a crisis, since "preventive" counseling often helps students *stay* mentally healthy and productive. It takes much less time and energy to resolve a problem before it gets out of hand. If your child is having difficulties in school, with peers, or with unusual stress, a counselor can help bring the problem into awareness and into focus. That's half the battle.

If your child is exhibiting any of the warning signs described earlier in this chapter, the time to get help is now. But where can you go to find it? Although counselors should be available as early as elementary school, they seldom are. Check into your child's school to learn what resources are available. If it doesn't provide counseling services, or if counseling time is so limited that help is minimal, you may need to seek outside assistance.

Unfortunately, some people still feel there's a stigma attached to seeing a counselor—or a "shrink." If your child had a reading problem, would you hesitate to see a reading specialist? A counselor, like a reading specialist, is someone who can genuinely help your child. A trained outsider can see problems you may not be able to see because you're too close to them. A counselor can also provide you with reassurance that you're doing okay as a parent. And your child will come away with tools she can use to recognize and solve problems, make better choices, raise her self-esteem, and feel more confident about herself and her place in the world.

You can get counseling from a *psychiatrist,* a *psychologist,* a *psychiatric social worker,* or a *family therapist.* All have different degrees and different types of training and experience. In shopping for a counselor, start by asking friends or school officials for suggestions. The school psychologist or gifted program coordinator may have some resources to share. Your family doctor or pediatrician may be able to recommend someone. You can also contact your local county department of mental health and your local chapter of the Mental Health Association for referrals.

Be sure to check your insurance ahead of time, especially if you can't afford to pay for counseling yourself. Be prepared, however: few policies cover more than a portion of mental health services. And some insurers may insist that you use only the counselors on their approved list.

Before you make the first appointment, it's wise to find out how the counselor feels about issues that are critical to you. What are his or her views on giftedness? Does he or she have experience working with gifted and talented kids? Look for someone who seems relaxed, confident, knowledgeable, and supportive. If you feel comfortable with this person, chances are your child will, too.

Some professionals may suggest that the entire family come in for counseling. Keep an open mind: this can't hurt, and it almost certainly can help. Some children may feel better about counseling if other family members are present. On the other hand, teens are often *less* communicative when their parents are around, so therapists will usually see a teen alone first for a few sessions to build trust, then invite the family in when everyone agrees.

What's most important is to choose someone with whom your child feels safe. When this is the case, real helping can happen, and it won't be long before everyone feels the effects.

●   ●   ●   ●   ●   ●   ●   ●   ●   ●

READ MORE ABOUT IT

To find out more about the ideas in this chapter, read:

Directory of American Youth Organizations: A Guide to Over 400 Clubs, Groups, Troops, Teams, Societies, Lodges, and More for Young People by Judith B. Erickson, Ph.D. (Free Spirit Publishing, 1990; updated every other year). Lots of information about all kinds of clubs for young people—and possible contacts for gifted kids looking for others who share their interests,

Fighting Invisible Tigers: A Stress Management Guide for Teens by Earl Hipp (Free Spirit Publishing, 1985). Specific stress-management and life-management skills for young people.

A Parent's Guide to Eating Disorders by Brett Valette (Avon, 1988). Vital information for concerned parents. Or write: The National Association of Anorexia Nervosa and Associated Disorders, Inc., Box 271, Highland Park, IL 60035.

Perfectionism: What's Bad About Being Too Good? by Miriam Adderholdt-Elliott, Ph.D. (Free Spirit Publishing, 1987). Written for young people, this book can also teach adults a great deal about this common problem.

The Power of the Family by Michael P. Nichols (Fireside, 1988). A novel-like depiction of a troubled family and how therapy helps them.

Stick Up For Yourself! Every Kid's Guide to Personal Power and Positive Self-Esteem by Gershen Kaufman, Ph.D., and Lev Raphael, Ph.D. (Free Spirit Publishing, 1990). Encouraging how-to advice on being assertive, building relationships, and becoming responsible. For ages 8 and up.

The Survival Guides for Adolescence series by Gail C. Roberts, B.Ed., M.A. and Lorraine Guttormson, M.A. (Free Spirit Publishing, 1990). This personal growth series includes *You and Your Family, You and School,* and *You and Stress,* hands-on workbooks that help kids identify, address, and solve problems. A *Leader's Guide* gives suggestions for introducing, discussing, and enriching the activities.

Teaching Children Self-Discipline at Home and at School by Thomas Gordon, Ph.D. (Times Books/Random House, 1989). An excellent discussion of why traditional rewards, punishment, and praise do more harm than good, plus non-controlling methods to get kids to change their behavior.

●　　●　　●　　●　　●　　●　　●　　●　　●　　●

CHAPTER 5

Programming for the Gifted

I T TAKES A LOT OF TIME TO BE A GENIUS,
YOU HAVE TO SIT AROUND
SO MUCH DOING NOTHING,
REALLY DOING NOTHING.

GERTRUDE STEIN

How can your child's educational needs be met?

How can you influence the gifted program
at your child's school?

When Paul was in the first grade, he learned rapidly. He could read and do math at a fifth-grade level, but no one knew that. His behavior in class was totally unpredictable. His papers were sloppy. He rarely paid the slightest attention to the rules of the classroom and the schoolyard. He was inattentive and disruptive, making comments under his breath and distracting those around him. Sometimes he crawled around on the floor or jabbed other kids with a pencil.

At home, Paul's parents were in awe of his intelligence, and they had all but given up trying to get him to behave. He was allowed to "run" the household, with few rules or restrictions placed on him.

Finally Paul's teacher referred him to the school psychologist as being "behavior disordered." She expected that Paul would be placed in a special "behavior disordered" class. The psychologist, however, uncovered Paul's giftedness and realized that his behavior was a reaction to an inappropriate education.

The teacher was made to recognize that Paul had potential. She gave him more challenging and interesting work, sometimes on an individual basis. The psychologist also showed Paul's parents how to get involved in a positive way. Knowing that his parents and teacher were in the same arena helped Paul to understand that people were taking care of him and really trying to meet his needs. His disruptive behavior lessened dramatically.

Research tells us that gifted and talented kids often learn in a different way and at a different rate than children of more average abilities. They are also distinct individuals, so some of them may excel in language yet take twice as long to do their math. That's why the standard school curriculum doesn't meet their educational needs. The whole point of gifted education is to provide these children with appropriate educational opportunities so they can reach their potential.

Why should you, as a parent, care about what goes on in your child's school? Because bright children who are bored and frustrated in school are in danger of dropping out—mentally, physically, and emotionally. They may rebel, turn into "problem children," be punished for smarting off, or become "class clowns." They may learn to underachieve. If they never have to do anything that's challenging, they often end up with poor or nonexistent study skills.

It's critical for gifted kids to develop *self*-teaching skills, which they will use throughout their lives. All along the line, there will be times when they will be able to surpass their teachers' knowledge, if they know how to do research and especially how to learn.

If you enjoyed watching your preschooler get excited by learning, it would be heartbreaking to see her lose that early enthusiasm. Children may have a general sense of being bored and frustrated without knowing why. They don't realize that part of the reason is because they learn at such a rapid rate. They don't have the ability to figure out what's going on, but we as adults do. Appropriate gifted programming can ensure that your child stays excited about learning, the world, and her own possibilities.

GIFTED OR "DUMB"?

SOME CHILDREN HAVE NO CONCEPT of their own high ability. They know they are different from their age peers—some realize this at a very early age—but they don't know why they're different, so they often come to negative conclusions. They may start to think of themselves as "stupid" or "weird." They lack the emotional maturity to understand that just because they learn differently or faster, this doesn't mean they can't get along with anybody. It's our job as parents and teachers to get across the message that they are *not* weird, and that being gifted is a positive thing.

A four-year-old once told me, "I'm really dumb." I asked him what he meant by "dumb." "Well," he told me, "dumb means different. I don't think like everybody else." He had a tremendously large vocabulary that set him apart. He would make comments like, "That's really preposterous." Hardly "dumb"—but definitely different!

Doing well in school is no guarantee that your gifted child's potential is being fulfilled. In fact, a kid who's getting straight A's may not be learning very much. You may feel good when your child comes home with straight-A papers, but think again. Is your child being sufficiently challenged? Is he being made to master new material, or is he just going over material he already knows? Is he having to make an effort, or is he breezing by?

Many bright kids can do the required work easily and have no trouble meeting the teacher's basic expectations. The fact that they could be doing so much more often goes unnoticed, particularly if they are well-behaved. Unless they have the chance to work with more advanced materials, their true abilities stay hidden.

One of the problems for gifted kids is that in the typical classroom, the pressure—especially peer pressure—is on conforming and "fitting in." If their school work is repetitive, they see it as information they already have and don't really need. And if they're especially productive, they may end up with more of the same kinds of assignments, rather than fewer or different ones. And who wants to do busy work? No wonder so many of them catch on quickly (after all, they're fast thinkers) and slow down so they're more like the average kids in their class.

Younger gifted kids who can't or won't conform to the average level of expectations may simply withdraw. In a sense, they become mental dropouts from learning. While many continue to pursue their education outside of school, through enrichment programs or their own self-directed projects, the pattern has been set: As far as the school is concerned, they are underachievers who have lost their desire to learn.

One 12-year-old gifted girl put it this way: "In a typical school day I whiz through my 'extra' classes and plod through the normal ones. Teachers repeat and 'go over one more time' and explain until their once-fresh ideas are almost meaningless. At times, I try to block it out and then get reprimanded for not paying attention. Sometimes it's easier to just let the haze creep over my eyes and reply robot-like. But it scares me—sometimes I feel like I'll never come back."

For all of these kids—different, bored, ignored, withdrawn, underachieving, and in a daze—gifted programming can be a big help. This chapter presents a number of models for special kinds of education aimed at the gifted and talented. It also suggests some ways you can start having meaningful input into your child's school experience.

PARENTS PRAISE GIFTED PROGRAMS

Father of a fourth grader:

"Before the gifted program, there was no need for her to attend school—she already knew all the material."

Mother of a fifth grader:

"Aaron was previously getting C's and B's and didn't like school and was bored. Now, in the gifted program, he's getting much better grades and he loves school."

Father of an eighth grader:

"Danny seems less bored and has to work considerably more, now that he's in the gifted program. I believe he was just coasting along before."

Parent of a third grader and an eighth grader:

"The gifted program makes school more interesting, so my children are more motivated to attend."

MAKING SCHOOL BETTER FOR GIFTED KIDS

NO SINGLE CURRICULUM MODEL is perfect for all children, gifted or otherwise. What's best will vary by educational system and individual student. But whichever system is selected, it must be based on the needs, abilities, and talents of the children who will be taking part in it.

The regular school curriculum can be adjusted for gifted kids in a number of ways. Some schools group students by ability, in a sort of school-within-a-school, while some districts set up separate magnet schools for gifted children. Magnet schools are a particularly effective solution, since bright children get to spend all day with others as bright as they are, instead of just being gifted on Tuesdays at 9 o'clock.

In some schools, gifted kids are clustered within a regular class. Then the teacher gives them enrichment opportunities beyond the usual curriculum, such as special projects. As always, it's up to the teacher whether the children will feel singled out in a negative way, or whether they will benefit from the extra attention.

Following is a rundown of some of the methods used today in gifted programming. They may be offered singly or in combination.

Acceleration

Commonly known as "skipping a grade," acceleration allows your child to jump to a higher level of class work than her age would ordinarily dictate. The jump can be for a particular class, or she can skip an entire grade. This method is usually considered when a student can work at a level two or three years beyond other students her age.

Acceleration can happen in more than one way: by early entry to first grade, in a self-contained gifted classroom, with credit by examination, by literally skipping a grade, or with concurrent enrollment in both college and high school.

While acceleration is reasonably commonplace, many people have been against it. They worry that if a gifted child starts rubbing elbows with older kids, she'll "suffer emotionally." They raise points worth thinking about. If your youngster skips one of the early grades, what may be the results when high school rolls around and she's the youngest among her peers? She may not be as large physically, which can affect her participation in sports activities. She won't start to drive when her friends do, and she may not be ready to date at the same time as her schoolmates.

Despite these considerations, there hasn't been a single study showing that kids who skip have greater problems than kids who don't. On the contrary, many studies show that when children are allowed to learn at their own pace, they feel better about themselves, they're more motivated and creative, they have higher aspirations, and they're more socially "with it."

Enrichment Programs

These are designed to replace or extend the regular school curriculum. The goal of enrichment should be to help your child work on higher level skills, such as divergent and evaluative thinking, problem-solving, and creativity. Some of the ways these skills can be taught are through debates and discussions, research, or simulations.

Enrichment can be added by using a *resource room* (described in the next section), hiring specially trained teachers, inviting community professionals in to teach or make presentations, or setting up individual projects or contracts with the student. Enrichment programs vary from an hour a week to an hour or more a day, or even a whole semester a year in some schools.

Many states have also offered special seminars, field trips, and mini-courses to add enrichment for gifted students. "Future Problem Solving Bowl" and similar competitions are another form of gifted enrichment. In this state and national contest, begun by Dr. Paul Torrance in 1975, teams of students are given a problem to solve. The students do research, list subproblems, and present solutions orally and in writing. For more information about Future Problem Solving Bowl, write: FPSB, P.O. Box 98, Aberdeen, NC 28315, or call (919) 944-4707.

Resource Rooms

Resource rooms are usually libraries or other specially equipped rooms that gifted kids use at the teacher's discretion. Perhaps when the student has completed a particular assignment, he may be allowed to go to the resource room to look up or research something or work with the librarian or other specialist.

Resource rooms can be havens for gifted kids—places where they can make new friends of similar abilities, work on fascinating projects, and use special equipment. Usually the teacher who works in these special rooms is sensitive to the needs of the gifted and talented and is not threatened by students who often know more than he or she does about certain things.

Sometimes, however, if the use of the resource room is entirely up to the classroom teacher, students who could benefit may never get sent there. And some may be able to use it only at the teacher's discretion—as in "You can't go to the resource room today because you mouthed off in class." Ideally, resource rooms shouldn't be used as either punishments or rewards. They should be available to students who need them.

Pull-Out Programs

These are part-time enrichment programs that remove gifted kids from the regular classroom. They usually provide special activities not offered in the regular classroom. For example, some deal with emotional and social competencies or thinking skills not related to instruction in a particular discipline. Pull-out programs can vary from an hour a week to several hours a day, though the latter is rare.

Once enrichment pull-out programs have been established, careful attention and extra effort are required for them to be effective. When they don't work, it's usually because they keep students busy with irrelevant activities. Also, districts that start with a pull-out program are unlikely to develop more comprehensive gifted programming later on.

Another drawback of pull-out programs is that students may miss out on important or fun events that happen in their regular classroom. What if there's a test the next day on material presented while they were in the pull-out program? Will they always miss recess or special programs? If so, then the gifted program is more of a pain than a pleasure, and children won't be motivated to stay in it for long.

Mentorships

In a mentorship, a gifted student is paired with an adult or other student who's an expert in a particular subject or profession. Mentors come from either the academic or business community. Usually, students and mentors agree to work together closely for a set period of time. Meetings are arranged during or after school hours as determined by the participants.

Accelerated and enriched learning are the natural consequences of mentorships. They also provide good career exploration opportunities.

Independent Study

A student doing an independent study is allowed to work at her own pace on a program of her own choosing. A mentor or teacher serves as a guide.

Most independent study programs require the student to develop a plan stating the subject of the study, list her goals and objectives, plan activities to achieve her goals, and complete a final product. The study plan may take the form of a contract.

Advanced Placement

Advanced Placement classes—called AP classes—offer gifted high schoolers greater academic challenge, more opportunities for accomplishment, and chances to make individual progress.

AP classes are college-level classes taught by qualified high school teachers on the high school campus. They may take the form of an honors class, a strong regular class, or an independent study. AP classes let student avoid repeating work they've already done.

Internships

Another way for bright high school students to enhance their education is through internships—working with professionals on the job. Internships are usually available only to high school students in the later grades.

MORE PRAISE FOR GIFTED PROGRAMS

Parent of a junior high student:

"In the fourth grade of our neighborhood school, when my son was the first to have his work done, he would be given more busy work to do, which he resented. Once he was in the gifted program, everyone was working more closely at the same pace and he felt more comfortable—not singled out for being capable."

Mother of a first grader:

"Because of the gifted program, I've noticed that my daughter has increased her problem-solving and analytical skills. Also, due to the enrichment opportunities and the diversity of socioeconomic groups represented in the classroom, she's developed an interest in and enthusiasm for experiences in nature, art, and other cultures. She has a much more well-rounded, accurate view of the world than I think she could get anywhere else."

Father of a sixth grader:

"My son's behavior and attitudes towards school changed as he became interested in learning. He looks forward to school. Before participation in the gifted program, he was becoming bored with school."

Mother of a ninth grader:

"He seems more interested in the 'process' of learning. Also, his approach to problems seems better—he looks at all sides in seeking solutions."

YOUR RIGHTS AND WHAT'S RIGHT

PARENTS HAVE THE RIGHT to know exactly how children are being identified for their school's gifted program. You also have the right—and the responsibility—to know when tests are being given, and what the results are. That way you can talk about these tests with your child so he'll feel more comfortable with what's happening to him.

You must be informed if your child is participating in a gifted class. Some districts hesitate to tell parents for fear they will get inflated egos. But you *need* to know so you can understand and support your child.

Since gifted education is so new in our country, the curriculum of teacher education programs in many cases hasn't caught up. So teachers themselves aren't always sure of how to make gifted education appropriate to the needs of gifted kids. Don't hesitate to ask questions and speak up for your child. Chapter 6 gives you some advocacy tips that should come in handy.

How do you know whether what your school provides is right for your child? Visit, visit, visit! Not in a threatening way, but by saying to the teacher, "I have some time—is there something I can help you with? Something I could do in the classroom? I'd like to read a story to the kids; can I share my hobby with the class?"

With my own three children, I found that if I wrote some positive comments to the teacher at the beginning of the year about things I liked that he or she was doing in the class, I felt that gave me the right to gripe later on when things weren't going altogether positively. I'm sure this approach put me on a better footing with the teacher.

TOWARD A BETTER CURRICULUM

A GOOD GIFTED CURRICULUM considers the students' unique characteristics, needs, and interests. It provides them with a more profound educational experience.

Traditionally, gifted and talented youngsters are provided with more of the same work or busy work when they complete their regular work, but these options don't help them. Activities that reward the child—like coloring, being teacher's helper, playing a game, or helping slower children—aren't really rewards. They miss the point and don't meet the child's intellectual needs.

Gifted programs shouldn't be regarded merely as supplements to regular programs, but as alternatives that retain certain elements of a regular program. Skill work in basic subject areas is necessary, of course. Basic skills—reading, writing, computing—need to be taught with materials at the gifted child's level. Materials may need to be adapted to reduce repetition. A good program affords plenty of chances for creative application and critical thinking.

Independent study is one way to incorporate skill work while developing higher level thinking skills. In a nutshell, there's a big difference between memorizing a fact and knowing how to apply it creatively. The program also can be made different (and better) by making it more complex, faster-moving, and more meaningful to the students.

Differentiation can occur in these four areas:

1. Content. The subject matter or material to be covered may be altered to allow for abstractness, complexity, variety, or organization. Teachers can organize the material so it will help gifted kids discover or develop some basic idea. This capitalizes on the excitement and curiosity of bright students.

Content may also be altered by moving faster through the material, or going deeper into the area of study. For example, the mathematically gifted child might cover a year's worth of math in a semester. With the extra time, he might study different number base systems, number patterns, or an abstract concept that the child of more average ability may not grasp.

Or, when studying her city, a child might choose to look at other cities and discuss issues in city planning and development, perhaps creating a plan for an ideal city.

2. Process. Learning means using your brain, learning how to think, and learning how to deal with frustration. The learning process spells out how learning is supposed to take place—how the content will be studied, what thinking skills will be used, and how skills will be acquired. It can mean forming a hypothesis, testing and proving (or disproving) a theory, and doing research. Open-endedness, discovery, and emphasis on reasoning may be stressed.

Teachers can allow students the freedom to choose which method they will use to solve a problem, or to come up with their own methods.

3. Product. Gifted kids can use different ways to demonstrate what they've learned. Too often, the usual product is a paper or a test. But it can be an invention, a solution to a problem, a new game, a video, a play, and so on.

4. Learning environment. Learning settings can be varied in many ways—for example, by moving students to a different location, calling in a teaching specialist, or blending classrooms. The learning environment needs to include appropriate equipment and facilities—essentials like language and science laboratories, computer terminals, videotaping equipment, and so on.

The learning atmosphere should be one of mutual trust, respect, and commitment to self-improvement. The climate the teacher creates should encourage thinking and questioning, respect individual differences, and allow for disagreement and controversy. It must be a safe place where a student can take risks without fear of failure or humiliation.

Finally, the learning environment must be responsive to gifted kids' feelings as well as their intellectual needs. When this is the case, children can accept constructive criticism, respond creatively, and develop ways to cope in the real world.

A differentiated curriculum may extend or study in depth an existing subject area, or shift to an area that arises out of the student's own interests. Either approach can emphasize higher-level thinking skills.

Independent study is another way to involve gifted students in planning, carrying out, and evaluating their own work. Teachers need to make sure that the child's interests are the starting point, but that the child is not simply "doing his own thing." The curriculum needs to be well planned, conscientiously carried out, and accurately evaluated.

Regular evaluation is essential as a basis for refining, modifying, and recycling any gifted program. This is where your input as a parent is especially valuable. Whether it's formal (as written evaluations) or informal (as ongoing comments to the teacher and principal), your constructive ideas for improving the program are vital and should be welcomed.

Gifted kids need to interact with other gifted kids. Part of the benefit of any gifted program is that it allows bright youngsters to spend time with and make friends with others like themselves. Group discussions and brainstorming sessions help kids develop higher level thinking skills.

The downside is that your child's best friend may not live in your neighborhood. Talented kids like to study together, work on projects together, and just hang out together. Driving, car pooling, or other transportation will then be a fact of life. But when your child feels good about herself because she finally fits in with her equally gifted friends, the driving will be worth it.

STILL MORE PRAISE FOR GIFTED PROGRAMS

Parent of sixth and ninth graders:

"I think the best thing about being in the gifted program is the exposure to all the other bright kids and their ideas."

Parent of a fifth grader:

"She feels more challenged by being with others who think on her level, and by working with teachers who appreciate her talents and are trained to work with these kids. Everyone benefits."

Parent of a high school boy:

"Len feels like part of a select group and therefore puts forth more effort than he would in an ordinary school setting."

Parent of a fourth grader:

"Mike doesn't complain anymore that school is boring. He has more friends of similar intellectual level and interest level and is happy about that. He's not afraid to show his intellectual abilities in front of the other boys."

Father of two children in gifted programs:

"Perhaps the best I can say is what the gifted program has not done—it has not conditioned the creative spirit out of our children. It has given them the self-confidence to take reasonable risks without fear of failing."

WHAT ARE TEACHERS FOR?

WHATEVER CURRICULUM MODEL or strategies a school selects, the staff has to be involved in the planning stages. The administration, teachers, and students should work together to develop, implement, and evaluate the curriculum.

The teacher's role is to create a learning environment that's both safe and stimulating, and to help the students achieve a balance between small and large group and independent activities. The teacher serves as a facilitator rather than as a dispenser of information, while maintaining a focus on the quality of the learning experiences.

While your input as a parent should be considered and valued, you need to remember that when it comes to actual implementation of the curriculum—the day-to-day reality of teaching—the teacher has the final word. It's the teacher who is the trained professional.

When you're ill, you see a doctor, and you rely on his or her judgment to give you the right prescription or treatment to cure your illness. In the educational community, the teacher is the doctor, prescribing the curriculum that best suits the child. We may at times need the help of other specialists if the prescription isn't working, but the teacher deserves to be regarded as the professional in charge. Parents do, however, have the right—and the responsibility—to ask questions and insist on appropriate educational programming for their children.

A good teacher of gifted kids must have a desire to teach students who may be even brighter than he or she is. The teacher had better love learning and have confidence in his or her abilities to work with students.

When bright students were asked to describe a "gifted" teacher, they listed these characteristics:

▶ someone who understands and respects gifted kids,

▶ someone who encourages kids to set and achieve high goals,

▶ someone who goes into assignments deeper than the book,

▶ someone who writes compliments on a student's paper
  if he or she does a good job,

▶ someone who is responsible, efficient, and smart, and

▶ someone who is loving and caring.

HOW PARENTS FEEL ABOUT GIFTED TEACHERS

Parent of a third grader:

"My child had a very rough year in second grade in a traditional classroom with a teacher who had little apparent ability or opportunity to encourage her. She has blossomed and been happy and challenged in the gifted program."

Parent of a fourth grader:

"Her gifted teachers make her more at ease. They don't expect the same answer from everyone."

Parent of a seventh grader:

"Previously, our daughter was bored with the lack of educational material offered to above-average students in our regular program. Now she's learning more, and is enthusiastic about her classes. Her teachers make sure she can keep learning instead of being held back while the others catch up."

It takes more time for a teacher to plan and evaluate lessons for gifted students. Many professionals and parents wrongly believe that teaching smart kids is easy because they learn faster and easier than the average child. Nothing could be further from the truth!

Gifted and talented children require *more* teacher time because of the quantity of work they do, and *more* teacher training because of the sophistication and quality of that work. Just by realizing this, you can be a big help to your child's teacher.

If you've got any time at all, offer to help in or out of the classroom. Some ways to help include offering to drive on field trips, doing outside research, making helpful classroom teaching aids, and working with small groups of children on enrichment activities such as reading.

BORED NO MORE

Educator Judy Galbraith has identified one of the "Great Gripes" of gifted kids as "School is too easy and it's boring." Students had the following suggestions for making school more challenging:

★ "I ask teachers if I can do something else when I already know the assignment. I try to have something specific in mind so they know I'm not going to just slough off. Most of the time they don't object."

★ "Reading is my salvation. I ask to go to the library every chance I get. Most of the time, it's OK with teachers."

IT'S A MATCH!

WHAT HAPPENS when gifted kids and gifted programs match—when the curriculum meets the children's needs? Here's what parents have said:

▶ "My child feels challenged."

▶ "My child has developed self-confidence and is now motivated."

▶ "My child LOVES school and learning."

▶ "The classes are work, but fun too."

▶ "No longer is my child ridiculed for being a 'know-it-all.' She is with other kids who think on the same level. She has an easier time being accepted and making friends."

READ MORE ABOUT IT

To find out more about the ideas in this chapter, read:

The Colorado Handbook for Parents of Gifted Children, edited by Julie Gonzales (Colorado Association for Gifted and Talented, 1988).

The Gifted Kids Survival Guide (For Ages 11-18) by Judy Galbraith (Free Spirit Publishing, 1983).

Managing the Social and Emotional Needs of the Gifted by Connie Schmitz and Judy Galbraith (Free Spirit Publishing, 1985).

CHAPTER 6

Advocacy: Working for Improvement

S UCCESS IS KNOWING THE DIFFERENCE
BETWEEN CORNERING PEOPLE
AND GETTING THEM IN YOUR CORNER.

BILL COPELAND

How can I speak up for my child?

How can I go about getting more support and funds
for gifted programs and kids?

If you want to make sure that your gifted child receives the best education possible, *get involved in supporting gifted education.* Otherwise the massive educational bureaucracy will just go on slogging along in the same old, timeworn grooves.

Become an advocate rather than an adversary. An advocate is one who pleads someone's case, and you'll get much better results this way than if you think of yourself as going up against an enemy.

It's a fact of life that our society is sometimes biased against bright people. But if we would only think about it, the direction to take becomes obvious: We are all best served if *every* child is educated to achieve his or her full potential. Yet teachers and administrators who support gifted education are in the minority of their profession. We parents must become advocates, since we have the wisdom and knowledge it takes to fight for our children.

Where to begin? First of all, keep informed about what's going on in your child's school. Become as active at the school or in the PTA as you possibly can, since this is a good way to learn what's happening both inside and outside the classroom. Help out in your child's classroom whenever you can, and offer to share one of your talents or hobbies with the class.

Don't hesitate to question everything you're told about gifted education. Surprisingly, not all that's labeled gifted *is* gifted or, for that matter, is even educationally sound. Besides, by becoming active, you'll be a terrific role model for your child. Actions really do speak louder than words.

ADVOCACY ON THE LOCAL LEVEL

AS A PARENT, you're part of the single largest power-wielding group in the school system, more powerful than teachers or administrators. Our schools are a reflection of our society, and you're a vital part of that society.

Without parent advocacy and participation, our gifted programs literally wouldn't survive. More than half of the gifted programs within local districts are there because of gifted kids' parents. Moms and dads working in a non-threatening way with teachers, administrators, and school boards have successfully brought about major changes in their children's school settings.

Dorothy Knopper is an excellent example of such parent advocacy. Along with a small group of parents, Dorothy pushed for individualized education and a special curriculum for the gifted and talented. The group was instrumental in developing an exemplary gifted program which is in place today in Livonia, Michigan. On the state level, Dorothy's advocacy led to the Michigan legislation funding gifted education in 1974, as well as the hiring of a state consultant for the gifted.

But you don't have to get *that* involved! *Any* time you put into improving the system is bound to benefit your child. So let's get started on the nuts and bolts of what you can do.

HOW TO BE HEARD: BEGIN WITH THE TEACHER

FOR A GIFTED PROGRAM to be successful, everyone must cooperate and even compromise a little. If your child's gifted program turns out not to be truly different from the regular program, or the teacher simply isn't an effective one, you need to speak up for your child.

It helps to know your school district's "philosophy statement" regarding gifted education. Nearly all school districts have such a statement, and once you're familiar with it, you can use it as ammunition in your efforts to get your child's school to implement better programming.

School systems are highly structured organizations. It's generally best to start at the bottom and work your way to the top. For example, let's say you see a problem with your child's homework—she's been given too much of the same thing. If she can master a particular concept in five problems, but the assignment is to do 50 of them, or if she's supposed to write her spelling words 20 times even though she already knows the list, it's time for you to communicate with your child's teacher.

But no matter what, if your child is having difficulty with a teacher, start with that teacher, not the superintendent! In fact, if you contact someone higher up, he or she will usually ask you if you've spoken with the teacher. Even if you think you know what the teacher's response will be, go there first. If you don't feel satisfied, go to the principal then—but never before trying the teacher.

Some school districts have coordinators of gifted services. Although they usually have heavy workloads and little free time, they may be friendly to your cause. Gifted coordinators have an overall picture of the programming for the district and of the needs of gifted and talented students. They also may have some powers of persuasion.

If your district doesn't have someone specifically designated as the program coordinator for gifted education, the director of special education may be the best source of information. Subject area or curriculum coordinators may provide help. If you can find an advocate within the system, you're more likely to be listened to than if you speak up alone.

Other parents with knowledge of the system and its workings can also be an asset. If you're new at the school or feel a bit intimidated by the establishment, get another parent to become involved along with you.

TEN TIPS FOR TALKING TO TEACHERS

1. Make an appointment to meet and talk.

2. If you know others who feel the way you do, consider going to the teacher together.

3. Think through what you want to say *before* you go into your meeting with the teacher.

4. Choose your words carefully.

5. Don't expect the teacher to do all of the work or come up with all of the answers.

6. Be diplomatic, tactful, and respectful.

7. Focus on what you need, not on what you think the teacher is doing wrong.

8. Don't forget to listen.

9. Bring your sense of humor.

10. If your meeting isn't the success you hoped it would be, move up a level and try talking to the principal. Follow steps 1-10 again. Keep moving up until you get some answers.

At times your emotions may get in the way of your intellect, and you may be tempted to strike out in unacceptable ways. Though your impatience with "the system" may be justified, tact is the key to getting your ideas across and accepted.

Pushy, obnoxious parents may do more harm than good. If you're really outraged, give yourself some time to cool off. Write your thoughts down, and keep them to yourself. Take a walk, burn off the excess energy, sleep on it. You want support, which you won't get if you alienate those with the power to bring about change.

If you *demand* gifted classes, you'll probably meet resistance. Instead, you'll get further by saying something like, "I know you're doing an excellent job in your classroom (school, school system). It must be very difficult to meet all the different needs and abilities of every student. You're trying to do all you can. But there's one thing you can't give your gifted and talented students, even if you're the best teacher (administrator, school board), and that's the opportunity for them to be together, to network and share ideas. They need that opportunity, and that's why they must leave your class, or have different work within your class, at least for some of the time."

TALK YOUR WAY TO THE TOP

When it comes to talking to teachers—or principals, or anyone else you approach for help for your child—a little diplomacy goes a long way. Here are some examples of styles to try (and to avoid):

Instead of this:	*Try saying this:*
"Why don't you have the gifted program in place? What's wrong with the administration?"	"I know that the gifted program is new and you need time to develop the curriculum, but what specifically will be done this year? And how can I help?"
"Why aren't you providing _____ for the gifted kids in our district?"	"You're doing an excellent job providing for gifted and talented students. I can tell you want to be on the cutting edge. For that reason, I thought you'd like to know about (what another district has done; an article I've read; a new idea; a resource person...)."
"Don't you know that this curriculum is outdated and inappropriate for my child?"	"How do you, the teacher (principal, superintendent, board member) feel about the district's curriculum? If you could make some changes, what would they be? Have you ever thought of _____?"

WORKING WITH
THE SCHOOL BOARD

SCHOOLS ARE A BUSINESS, yet they're essentially run by people who have little expertise in that particular business: school board members. School boards have the ultimate responsibility for decisions regarding the total curriculum, staff, and expenditures within each school district.

In general, board members are people who are elected from the community and dedicated to giving community service. Their time commitment is mammoth and admirable, with no pay, little recognition, and sometimes a lot of grief. They have been elected because they're concerned. But they may also have a personal axe to grind, or a favorite cause to push.

In working with school boards, it's helpful to know the members' backgrounds, and to be aware of their individual strengths and weaknesses. Campaign for those who hold ideals similar to yours and who speak up for gifted kids.

Attend a school board meeting. Know what's going on, and learn to ask appropriate questions. Seek out those who can be swayed, and do whatever you can to win them over to your side. At the same time, find out who the enemies to your cause are. Talk with them, too. Hear their arguments and ask if they'll listen to yours. See if you can't find something to agree on, or a point where you're willing to compromise. Don't waste valuable time and energy in arguments that only build hostility. Offer to serve on a task force or fact-finding committee.

GETTING SUPPORT FOR YOURSELF

AS THE PARENT OF A GIFTED CHILD, you may often feel stranded and alone. You are *not* alone! There are more than 2.5 *million* children in the United States alone who could be classified as gifted. They all have parents who probably have concerns and fears and hopes similar to yours. All you have to do is find a few.

You'll get a lot out of joining a parent support group. Such groups offer moral support, companionship, the chance to exchange ideas and increase your knowledge, and other adults who may join with you in advocating for your kids.

If your school district doesn't have a support group for parents of gifted students, start one. Contact the gifted program coordinator for help. He or she can give you the names of other parents of gifted students.

If your district doesn't have a gifted program coordinator, ask a teacher or principal for help. Start contacting other parents of gifted and talented youngsters. If there are parent groups in neighboring cities, connect with them. Find out how they got started, what problems they've encountered, what types of programs they have, and how they're supported (funds are needed for mailing costs, duplicating notices, refreshments, etc.). Find a place to hold a meeting and set the time. Post a notice at your local library, and be sure to tell the children's librarian. Contact your local newspaper in plenty of time to get a listing for the meeting.

GIFTED ADVOCACY GROUPS

These national organizations are good sources of information about gifted children, giftedness, gifted education, and more. They provide a variety of services including journals, conventions, and networking opportunities. Although these are primarily professional organizations—for theorists, educators, researchers, counselors, etc.—interested parents can benefit from getting involved.

A.E.G.U.S.
Association for the Education
  of Gifted Underachieving Students
P.O. Box 359
Bedford Hills, NY 10501

Association for the Gifted
Council for Exceptional Children
1920 Association Drive
Reston, VA 22091

Gifted Child Society
190 Rock Road
Glen Rock, NJ 07452

National Association for Gifted Children
1155-15th St. N.W., Suite 1002
Washington, D.C. 20005

In Canada:

Gifted Children's Association of British Columbia
PO Box 35177, Station E
Vancouver, British Columbia VGM 4G4

Ontario Association for Bright Children
2 Bloor St. West, Suite 100-156
Toronto, Ontario M4W 2G7

Assess the needs of other parents. You can do this formally through a school questionnaire (be sure to get the school's okay first), or informally by phone. Once you've compiled a list of the other parents' needs, you can set some guidelines for prospective programs.

Meetings should have a focus or topic so they don't turn into a brag session or a series of "ain't it awful" tales. Topics could revolve around concerns of parents regarding discipline, sibling rivalry, time management, program advocacy, etc. Speakers might include professionals who have a knowledge of gifted children, staff from a local university, or even a panel of gifted kids.

Be sure to allow time for just plain conversation. Usually some other parent has experienced the same or similar problems and is willing to share solutions or hindsight with the group.

Don't let it bother you if anyone outside the group accuses you and the other parents of being on an "ego trip." In my experience, the reverse is most often true. If anything, most parents try to play down their childrens' giftedness, and some actually go so far as to deny it.

Sometimes parents of bright kids have to make choices that may not be popular with relatives, neighbors, or friends. Others may disapprove if you decide to change schools, bus your child to a faraway school, educate him at home, or have him skip a grade, or if you choose to attend school board meetings. It's especially hard to stand up for your child when the disapproving voices are close and dear. At times like these, the support of a parent group or the empathy of another parent who understands can make all the difference in the world.

GETTING "THEM" MOVING ON THE STATE LEVEL

IN MOST CASES, local school districts cannot provide adequate gifted programming without state funds. In the vast majority of states, parents, parent groups, and associations are involved in advocacy for gifted education. To get involved yourself—or better yet, with a group of other parents of gifted kids—start by finding out who's eligible in your area to receive state money and under what conditions. (Any existing parent support group in your state can help you locate this information.)

In some states, local districts must compete for state grants. In others, money is given to schools that identify gifted pupils as prescribed by law. Other variations exist in which grants are given based on a variety of combinations of statistics. Find out also when the funding becomes available and how long it lasts. State gifted funds are voted upon by legislators who can often be swayed by phone calls and letters.

Here's a rundown of the legislative process for education bills, including gifted education bills, as it's followed in Illinois. Other states may use a similar process. Check with the legislator from your district. Legislators are the ones who introduce bills, but parents may educate legislators about gifted needs so bills addressing those needs stand a better chance of being introduced and passed.

1. The bill is reported to the floor of the house.

2. If the bill deals with money, it is assigned to the House Appropriations Committee.

3. The bill is assigned to the House Appropriations Sub-Committee on Education.

4. The Sub-Committee holds public hearings. Anyone can come and talk to the Sub-Committee about how they feel about gifted education. Amendments in the Sub-Committee can raise or lower gifted funding.

5. The bill is reported to the entire House Appropriations Committee, which can kill it or pass it to the entire House.

6. The bill is read twice on the floor of the House. Representatives can amend the amount of gifted funding up or down.

7. At the third reading, the House passes the bill and it goes on to the Senate. Or the House kills it, in which case there is no gifted funding.

8. If passed, the bill arrives in the Senate.

9. The Senate assigns the bill to the Appropriations Committee.

10. The Appropriations Committee has public hearings on the bill during the middle of May.

11. Amendments in the Committee can increase or decrease gifted funding.

12. At the third reading, the Senate votes for the bill and it goes on to the Governor, or kills it by voting the bill down.

13. If the bill goes to the Governor, he or she can:
    a. pass it,
    b. kill it, or
    c. use "amendatory veto power" to change it. For example, the governor might reduce the funding level for gifted education and pass the bill at a lower funding level.

14. If the bill passes, it becomes law.

15. On July 1 of that year, the local school district may learn how much money has been allocated to that year's gifted program.

As you can see, there are many places in this process where gifted funding can be increased, decreased, or totally cut.

Legislation concerning *how* to educate gifted kids is also important. It follows a similar process.

HOW'S YOUR STATE DOING?

WHEN THE COUNCIL of State Directors of Programs for the Gifted took a nationwide survey in 1987, it found that 25 states and Guam had mandated services for gifted education. The other 25 states and Puerto Rico didn't have such a mandate, although 22 states *allowed* such programs for the gifted. Delaware didn't have a mandate for services, but it had gifted programs in all of its school districts anyway. Vermont, New Hampshire, and Hawaii didn't have mandated services, nor did they support discretionary programs.

Seven state departments of education recommended a specific curriculum for gifted and talented students: Florida, Georgia, Hawaii, Kentucky, Ohio, Oklahoma, and West Virginia. Four states required a specific curriculum: Pennsylvania, Ohio, Kentucky, and Georgia.

How do different states define "gifted and talented?" General intellectual ability is the most common part of the definition in 46 states, as well as in Guam and Puerto Rico. (Only Nevada, North Dakota, Vermont, and Idaho don't include general intellectual ability in their definition.) In addition, 43 states include specific academic aptitude in their official definition.

States also vary in how they go about identifying gifted kids. Some *require* individual intelligence test scores, while many other states merely *recommend* using them. A few states *require* teacher input in order for a child to be identified as gifted, and a much greater number *recommend* it. Several states review the past products and accomplishments of students while considering whether they fit the definition of gifted and talented.

GETTING YOUR MESSAGE ACROSS

SO HOW DO YOU get your message across to the people who can take action? One of the best ways is by writing letters or telephoning your legislators.

It's only through our letters and phone calls that we can guarantee that gifted education will be taken seriously. Contact a local chapter of the League of Women Voters for information on locating the names, addresses, and phone numbers of the state legislators for your district.

Then either call your representatives at their local offices, or convey your message by letter. There may be a best time to write letters and make phone calls, which the League of Women Voters may be able to help you discover. In Illinois, it's between April 15 and May 15, since this is when House bills move to the floor of the House for voting, are passed on to the Senate for voting, and end up on the Governor's desk for signing.

The following samples should get you started.

FORM FOR LETTER TO LEGISLATOR

The Honorable Representative/Senator _____
State Capitol Building
City, State, ZIP

Date

Dear Representative/Senator _____:

Inform the legislator that:

1. You are a voting member of his or her district.

2. You are concerned about local gifted education in your legislative district.

Elaborate on the program your child participates in.

Tell the legislator what you want from him or her. For example:

1. "I would like you to vote (for/against) House Bill _____ (give the exact number of that year's bill)."

2. Say that you and others from this district are concerned.

3. Be specific about the action you'd like, including the amount of money the bill should have.

Finally, ask the legislator to send you a written reply to your letter, informing you of how he or she feels about the issue, and how he or she will vote.

SAMPLE LETTER TO LEGISLATOR

The Honorable Senator Bigbill
State Capitol Building
Springfield, IL 62706

April 20, 1991

Dear Senator Bigbill:

I am very concerned about gifted education in our Legislative
District 41. As a registered voter, I appreciated your positive
vote for Senate Bill 3065 last year. My local school, Bill Hill
School, has an excellent gifted program which my son John
Jr. enjoys very much. This program has really assisted my
son educationally.

At this point, I am writing you regarding HB 494, which
includes gifted funding between lines 22-29. Many of the
parents at Bill Hill School are concerned that the program
and our children's education will not be as good without the
state appropriation to our local district. I feel that the bill
should increase the amount of funding for gifted students to
$100 per child. This increase to $7.86 million on line 24 of
the bill would greatly assist our local district with supplies
and materials vital to the gifted program.

Would you please write to me, giving your views toward
gifted funding and your voting intention toward HB 494?

Sincerely yours,

_____

SAMPLE PHONE CALL SCRIPT

*Hello, my name is _____. I'm a registered voter
in Senator/Representative _____'s district.
I'm concerned about gifted legislation and how
Senator/Representative _____ will vote.*

*My son/daughter is in _____ school in the
_____ legislative/representative district.*

*I would appreciate a personal letter from
Senator/Representative _____ informing me
of his/her voting intentions in regards to HB #_____.
I feel that the bill should increase the amount of funding for
gifted students to $_____. This increase would
greatly assist our local district with supplies and materials
vital to the gifted program.*

*My name is spelled _____, and my address is
_____. I'd appreciate hearing from
Senator/Representative _____ prior
to the House/Senate vote on this bill.*

Thank you. Good-bye.

A FEW FINAL WORDS

IT'S NOT EASY TO RAISE *any* child, much less a curious, creative, intense gifted and talented child. But if you do your best to see that your child gets an excellent education, and hold on to your sense of humor while all about you are losing theirs, you *will* survive these challenging years. And your payoff will be one great kid. Good luck!

● ● ● ● ● ● ● ● ● ●

READ MORE ABOUT IT

To find out more about the ideas in this chapter, read:

Full Flowering: A Parent and Teacher Guide to Programs for the Gifted by Phyllis J. Perry (Ohio Psychology Publishing Co., 1985). Perry gives a comprehensive outline of programs and options for serving gifted students. She also includes a listing of advocacy groups and resources.

● ● ● ● ● ● ● ● ● ●

15 Questions Parents Ask—and 14½ Answers

SOME QUESTIONS DON'T HAVE ANSWERS, WHICH IS A
TERRIBLY DIFFICULT LESSON TO LEARN.

KATHERINE GRAHAM

1. What do I do if my child is an underachiever?

When you expect more from your child than you're getting, whatever his IQ, you're likely to perceive him as an "underachiever." This is actually a rather subjective label—meaning it's a matter of opinion.

One thing to consider is whether you're constantly pushing him to do more than he's comfortable doing. If he feels he can't possibly live up to your goals for him, no matter how hard he tries, he may simply stop trying. *Voilà*—an underachiever.

Some gifted kids resolve conflicts within themselves by mentally "dropping out." For example, if they want very much to be popular, they may hide their giftedness. This can happen if their peer group makes it clear that it's not "cool" to always get the best grades and come up with the right answers.

It turns out that underachieving can also be a good (but passive) way to get even with parents, especially near the teen years. "I know that ever since I was born, Dad has expected me to go to an Ivy League college and follow in his footsteps and be a lawyer, and I don't want to play the game," explains one young man. "I'm tired of the pressure." Counseling might help a family like this to confront some of its deeper issues.

I know a teenage girl who began underachieving so early that she never had a chance to be identified as gifted. Whenever she felt that anyone was getting close to her giftedness, she covered it up. There wasn't ever any doubt that she could do the work. She was able to ace advanced math after a few weeks in a summer course, after goofing off all during her senior year in high school. But she was mainly interested in being popular, and it wasn't "cool" to be gifted. Even counseling didn't help her, because when a child decides to dig in her heels, there isn't a lot that can be done about it. Kids ultimately have to make their own choices.

One thing you can do, especially with the creative underachiever, is to work with him on developing organizational skills. Help him to strike a balance between being creative and being organized. Some super-creative types seem to think that if they're organized and stick to a project until it's finished, this will take something away from their creativity. Show that it won't by modeling follow-through behavior on a creative project of your own.

2. What kinds of activities are best for my child at home?

You can apply some of what we've learned about good gifted programs to your child's everyday activities. For example, in order to help your child develop higher-level thinking skills, you might ask her to compare and contrast two stories or two different versions of the same story. Or read a story and leave the ending unfinished so she can complete it. Your child can practice evaluation by determining which story she likes better.

Even the hours spent watching TV can be educational if you encourage higher-level thinking instead of passive watching. For example, ask your child to compare and contrast two different programs, create a different ending to a program, or evaluate the worth of a particular program, series, or performance.

Suggest that your child group or classify her collections in different ways. Encourage her to think up different uses for household objects or new inventions to solve old problems (a better mousetrap?).

Even the young child should be allowed to decide if she'd rather wear the red sweater or the blue one. Be sure to ask why she made a particular choice. Her reasons may enlighten you and will prove thought-provoking for her.

Share your hobbies and interests with your child. Share the wonder of the world in the form of books, trips, and people. Look for historical points of interest, rocks, wiggly things, and new plant life. Discuss ideas.

Activities like cooking offer excellent opportunities for learning at home. The process includes reading and talking about the recipe, following the recipe, examining the ingredients, looking at how each is important, and, if one of the ingredients is missing, deciding what could be substituted and how this would change the recipe. Then you get to taste your creation. Suggested questions: Do you think this is a good recipe? Why? How could it be improved? What's your favorite food? Why?

3. My daughter is always saying she's bored at school. How can I tell if the work is inappropriate or if she's just lazy?

A lot of kids say their schoolwork is boring. Your daughter's work may really be boring and unchallenging, or she may be using this line as an excuse for not doing her homework or not performing up to her potential.

Start by talking to her teacher. Try to find out if the work is too easy, repetitive, or generally uninteresting. It's not likely that laziness is the problem, but maybe your daughter needs to learn some strategies for dealing with boredom.

I remember one kindergartner who always said, "I'm bored." I said to him, "I don't understand, there's all this stuff to do. What does bored mean to you?" He responded, "It means having to do what you want me to do rather than what I want to do." In other words, he was trying to get out of work that was assigned.

We need to explain to these kids that life is not always fun. Everyone gets bored at times, and there are always things we have to do that we don't want to do.

If your daughter complains about being bored when she's stuck waiting somewhere, you might teach her to fool around with mind games or puns or something else to keep her mind busy.

4. My very bright boy wants to read all the time. What should I do?

Let him read a great deal of the time, but also introduce him to the joys of going for a walk, playing a game, and playing with others. If you overreact or seem too worried or alarmed, you may force him into more of the same behavior. On the other hand, he needs to maintain a balance of physical and mental activity to stay healthy and to have a well-rounded life.

5. My very bright boy never wants to read anything but catalogs and how-to books about skateboards, remote-control cars, and kites. What should I do?

Get him books and magazines about those subjects. Some kids don't derive pleasure from what we call "pleasure reading." Maybe you need to share some books you've really liked, or even read aloud to him. But not everyone gets a kick out of fiction, and that's all right.

6. I think—no, I'm sure—that my child is smarter than I am. Is there anything special I need to know or do?

Although your child may have a higher IQ than you do, you've lived longer and have more wisdom. So you still need to be the one who's in control.

Don't be intimidated by an IQ, even if it's astronomical. If your child is interested in nuclear physics, you may never be able to keep up with what she learns. But there are other things she needs to know that you can help her with, such as tact, manners, and how to be socially acceptable. Perhaps you can share with her one of your hobbies or passions, whether it's singing or stamp collecting. Meanwhile, don't underestimate your own abilities. You'll always have something to teach your child.

7. One of my sons is gifted, the other isn't. Now what?

When two of my children were tested for giftedness during kindergarten, and one was identified gifted and the other wasn't, I chose not to have the first child placed in the gifted program because I didn't want one labeled and one not. Instead, I enrolled them both at an arts alternative magnet school. This solution catered to their creative bent and avoided the "one is, one isn't" problem.

Not long ago, identical 11-year-old twins applied to a New York City junior high school for the gifted and talented—and only one was accepted. Their grades were identical, but one girl was more talented in drama than the other. Their parents were very upset and vowed to fight the decision. The headline of the article in *USA Today* read, "Life's not fair, NYC twins learn."

You can help make life more "fair" for your kids by recognizing each child's uniqueness, which has nothing to do with IQ scores. Accentuate the specialness of each one. Since your gifted child is probably already getting special attention because of his giftedness, and is perhaps attending special classes, look for something his sibling excels at or is interested in, and take *him* for classes, too.

One caution: If you have a slow child and a gifted child, and you're always giving extra attention to the slow child to help him catch up, the gifted one may play down his gifts in order to get equal time from you. Make the effort to focus on your gifted child so he doesn't feel slighted.

8. How soon should I urge my daughter's school to test her for giftedness?

Some school districts now test as early as preschool. A few states mandate gifted programming for kindergarten through twelfth grade. Check into what's required in your state and what's available in your own district. If you suspect that your child was a gifted preschooler, but her kindergarten teacher doesn't seem to notice anything special about her, share your observations and feelings with the teacher.

9. How can I get my son to understand why "process" is important? He insists on putting only the answers down on his math papers, since it's so easy for him to figure out word problems in his head. But he won't go through the process or show his steps, even though the teacher demands it. And this affects his grades.

Try explaining to him that knowing *how* to do something is just as important as coming up with the right answer. Once he learns the steps necessary to figure out the answers to his word problems, he'll be better equipped for more advanced mathematical calculations.

Sometimes kids are graded down when they make mistakes during the computation stage, even though their final answers are correct. This may not seem fair to them, but it's important to show the process so the teacher can see their mistakes. If they consistently make errors in addition or multiplication, eventually they won't arrive at the right answers, once the problems get too complicated to do mentally.

10. Ever since my daughter entered puberty, she doesn't want to share any part of her social life with me. She used to tell me everything. How can I get back in touch with her?

What you're describing is the most natural process in the world. It's all part of your child's need to separate from you so she can become a fully independent adult.

Somewhere around puberty, when those devil hormones kick in, children decide that confiding in peers is safer and more fun than telling their parents all the fascinating details of their lives. Psychologists advise you to stay cool, keep sharing parts of your own life (if your child is interested), resist the temptation to pressure your child for information (or you'll get the opposite results from what you want), and don't take her need for privacy personally—it really doesn't have anything to do with you.

Be especially careful not to criticize when she *does* leak a detail or two about her life. And don't keep pushing for more and more on those rare occasions when she opens up a little. Just be a good listener. Many teenagers complain that their parents never listen to them when they do talk, so they no longer bother to talk. And be patient: If she used to tell you everything, one of these days, when the tumult of adolescence is past, she'll once again tell you *some* things.

11. Which is better for my gifted child—public school, or private school?

No one can answer that question for you. It depends on your child's individual needs, your family's values, your financial situation and willingness to sacrifice, and how good the schools are in your area, both public and private. And it depends on how good the gifted program is (or whether one even exists) at the particular school you're considering.

You'll need to do a great deal of investigating. Visit every school campus within miles around and ask a lot of questions. Ask everyone you know to share with you what they know about the schools their kids attend, but don't accept what someone else says without checking it out yourself.

If your local public school appears to have a responsive principal, an intelligently run gifted program, and teachers who care about children, there are certainly many advantages to sending your child there. If, however, you don't get a good feeling about any of these areas when you visit, you and your child might be happier at a private school. But only if it's a private school that has a responsive headmaster, creative programs that allow gifted and talented kids to do some independent learning, and teachers who truly care about—and understand—bright children.

12. How many after-school enrichment classes are too many for my child to take?

That depends on your child. One fourth-grader told me that he never wanted to take another extra class or lesson for as long as he lived. "But you're so good at everything," I pointed out. "That's just it," he answered. "Monday night's hockey, Tuesday night's swimming, Wednesday night's church, Thursday night's chess club. I have no time for myself!"

If you schedule your child's every waking moment, this robs him of self-directed time. Then, when he finally does have a free hour or two, he may claim to be "bored" because he doesn't know what to do with himself.

When my children were younger, I let them choose one outside activity for each grading period or semester. As the parent who had to do the driving, I needed to recognize my own limits, too. Just because you have a bright kid doesn't mean you won't have to say, "I know that you're interested in all these activities and classes, but I only have a certain amount of time and energy." Intense children are exhausting, and if you have more than one, they'll inevitably go in different directions.

13. What can I do about my obnoxious kid?

If by "obnoxious" you mean a "know-it-all" child who can't be told anything and has to have everything *her* way, it's time to take action! This is the kind of kid nobody wants to be around. She needs to learn how her behavior affects others. And she needs to become more sensitive to their needs, not just her own.

Sometimes it's difficult for these kids to hear, and your advice may be most noticeable if it's modeled. Show her what it's like to be on the receiving end of obnoxious or abrasive behavior. Say, "I'm going to show you what your behavior looks like. Then I want you to tell me how it feels to you." Give her an example and talk about it afterward.

Maybe your child's obnoxiousness is the result of ongoing power struggles between the two of you. If so, it's time for you to establish some good, fair, consistent rules—and stick to them no matter what. These will give your child a sense of security and a baseline for behavior, as well as the knowledge that someone older and wiser is in charge.

Generally speaking, a workable rule should:

▶ have a single interpretation. Agree on the details. For example, if you determine that "everyone must be ready for school before breakfast," define what you mean by "ready."

▶ be realistic. Is the rule enforceable? Can your child really obey it? Do you break the rule yourself? Are you in a position to check to see that the rule is followed?

▶ be open to discussion with your child. She needs to see why the rule is needed and how she might benefit by it.

▶ have consequences if it's not followed. What can your child expect if she breaks the rule?

14. What about me? When is it my turn?

Just as most gifted kids feel insecure from time to time, so do their parents! At times it may seem as if you're treading uncharted waters, stranded and alone. That's when you need other parents of bright children from whom you can grab a lifeline. Your own family members may not be the ones to turn to, since they may not understand what you're going through with your challenging child.

Seek out support from the parents of your kids' gifted friends. Parents have told me, over and over, "It's so comforting to know that other parents have kids who have read every book in the library, and they don't know what to do with them either." It helps to hear from other parents whose children have experimented with the gas stove, or torn apart the mantle clock to see how it works, or trained their cat to sleep in the bathroom sink. Mostly, it helps to know that you're not alone.

Parents, like other professionals, experience burn-out—it's just not as popular to admit it. Your social and emotional needs are important, too, and shouldn't be ignored. Here are some steps you can take to protect your own mental health:

▶ Have a life of your own. Develop your own hobbies and interests Take pride in your work.

▶ Be careful not to overinvest in your child. Living for him and through him isn't good for either of you.

▶ Take time for your creative self. Find ways to express your thoughts and feelings. Look for things you enjoy doing—things that make you feel renewed.

▶ Replace stressful thoughts with calming ones. Concentrate on the positive. Appreciate the good things going on around you and the people you care about.

▶ Have adult friends. This may sound obvious, but with the time commitments that gifted kids require, some parents don't allow themselves time to be with their own friends. Find friends who inspire you and give you energy.

▶ Seek and accept help when you need it. There are times when all of us face problems that are overwhelming. The help of a trained professional can put things into proper perspective.

15. Am I doing everything right for my child?

That's a BIG question! Here's half of an answer: Only *you* know for sure.

Hint: if you've read this far, you're a sincere, concerned parent who's *trying* very hard to do everything right. Anyway, perfectionism is a no-no. Why not give yourself an A?

MORE RECOMMENDED READING

IN ADDITION TO the "Read More About It" listings at the ends of the chapters, you may want to check out some of these helpful and informative resources. Many contain reading lists of their own, so you can keep following your curiosity and educating yourself for as long as you like.

Books

Halsted, Judith Wynn, *Guiding Gifted Readers* (Columbus, OH: Ohio Psychology Publishing Co., 1988). Halsted is a librarian who attempts to bring gifted children and books together. Her idea is to help gifted children, through books, to develop optimally as people. An annotated bibliography lists over 160 books.

Rimm, Sylvia, *How to Parent so Children Will Learn* (Watertown, WI: Apple Publishing Co., 1990). Based on her work at the Family Achievement Clinic, Dr. Rimm suggests some basic common-sense themes which can make significant differences in effective parenting. Dr. Rimm has also written *The Underachievement Syndrome.*

Saunders, Jacqulyn, and Pamela Espeland, *Bringing Out the Best* (Minneapolis, MN: Free Spirit Publishing, 1986). Geared to parents of children aged 2-7, this is a guide to the special needs of those children in different settings to assure that they will learn and thrive according to their abilities.

Smutny, Joan Franklin, Kathleen Veenker, and Stephen Veenker, *Your Gifted Child* (New York: Facts on File, 1989). Easily readable, filled with examples and advice, this book empowers parents to invite gifted development.

Vail, Priscilla, *Smart Kids with School Problems* (New York: E.P. Dutton, 1987). Too often, parents see and focus on the failure or problem, and may ignore or not recognize the child's talents. This book offers specific ways to find the roots of problems, suggests practical ways for dealing with them, and offers case studies of students who have been helped to succeed.

Webb, James, Elizabeth Meckstroth, and Stephanie Tolan, *Guiding the Gifted Child* (Columbus, OH: Ohio Psychology Publishing Co., 1986). This book provides a practical way to find knowledge, peace, and understanding for families with gifted children.

For some really "heavy reading"—and much meaty information—try these:

Bloom, B.S., editor, *Taxonomy of Educational Objectives. Handbook 1: Cognitive Domain* (New York: David McKay, 1956).

Cox, J., N. Daniel, and B. Boston, *Educating Able Learners: Programs and Promising Practices* (Austin, TX: University of Texas Press, 1985).

Krathwohl, D.R., B.S. Bloom, and B.B. Masia, *Taxonomy of Educational Objectives, Handbook II: Affective Domain* (New York: David McKay, 1964).

Maker, C.J., *Teaching Models in Education of the Gifted* (Rockville, MD.: Aspen Systems, 1982).

Periodicals

Advanced Development, A Journal on Adult Giftedness, PO Box 3489, Littleton, CO 80122.

The Gifted Child Quarterly, NAGC Headquarters, 1155-15th St. N.W., Suite 1002, Washington, D.C. 20005.

The Gifted Child Today, PO Box 637, 100 Pine Ave., Holmes, PA 19043.

Journal for the Education of the Gifted, The University of North Carolina Press, PO Box 2288, Chapel Hill, NC 27515-2288.

Roeper Review, A Journal on Gifted Education, Roeper City and County School, PO Box 329, Bloomfield Hills, MI 48013.

Understanding Our Gifted, Snowpeak Publishing, Inc., PO Box 3489, Littleton, CO 80122.

BIBLIOGRAPHY

Chapter 1

Bray, Jim, "The Governor's School of North Carolina," *G/C/T*, May/June 1979, p. 57.

Marland, S., *Education and the Gifted and Talented* (Washington, D.C.: Commission of Education 92nd Congress, 2nd Session, USCPO, 1972).

Terman, L.M., *Mental and Physical Traits of a Thousand Gifted Children. Genetic Studies of Genius*, Vol. 1 (Stanford, CA: Stanford University Press, 1947).

The 1987 State of the States Gifted and Talented Education Report (The Council of State Directors of Programs for the Gifted, 1987).

Chapter 2

Adler, Manfred, "Reported Incidence of Giftedness among Ethnic Groups," *Exceptional Children* 34:101-5, October 1967.

Alvino, James, Rebecca C. McDonnel, and Susanne Richert, "National Survey of Identification Practices in Gifted and Talented Education," *Exceptional Children* 48:124-32, October 1981.

Alvino, James, and Jerome Wieler, "How Standardized Testing Fails to Identify the Gifted and What Teachers Can Do About It," *Phi Delta Kappan* 61:106-9, October 1979.

Ciha, Thomas, Ruth Harris, Charlotte Hoffman, and Meredith Potter, "Parents as Identifiers of Giftedness, Ignored but Accurate," *Gifted Child Quarterly*, 191-195, Autumn 1974.

Delisle, James, and Judy Galbraith, *The Gifted Kids Survival Guide II* (Minneapolis: Free Spirit Publishing Inc., 1987).

Gallagher, James, *Research Summary on Gifted Child Education* (Illinois: Department for Exceptional Children, 1966).

Gardner, Howard, *Frames of Mind: The Theory of Multiple Intelligences* (New York: Basic Books, 1984).

Gonzales, Julie, editor, *The Colorado Handbook for Parents of Gifted Children* (Denver, CO: Colorado Association for Gifted and Talented, 1988).

Martinson, Ruth, *The Identification of the Gifted and Talented* (Ventura, CA: Office of the Ventura County Superintendent of Schools, 1974).

Masten, William G., "Gifted Minority Students: What the Research Suggests," *Roeper Review* 8:83-85, November 1985.

Mittan, Ken, *Teacher Pleaser or Potentially Gifted?* (LaHabra, CA: Foxtail Press Publishing, 1986).

Renzulli, Joseph S., "What Makes Giftedness? Reexamining A Definition," *Phi Delta Kappan* 60:180-84, 261, November 1978.

Torrance, E. Paul, "The Role of Creativity in Identification of the Gifted and Talented," *Gifted Child Quarterly* 28:153-56, Fall 1984.

VanTassel-Baska, Joyce, and Bernadette Strykowski, *An Identification Resource Guide on the Gifted and Talented* (Evanston, IL: Northwestern University, 1988).

Whitmore, Joanne R., "Recognizing and Developing Hidden Giftedness," *Elementary School Journal* 82:274-83, January 1982.

Whitmore, J.R., "Gifted Children can also be at Risk," *Teaching Exceptional Children* 20:4:10, 1988.

Chapter 3

Bloom, Benjamin, *Developing Talent in Young People* (New York: Ballantine Books, 1985).

Cassidy, Jack, and Carol Vukelich, "Not All Gifted Kids Read Early," *Gifted Children Newsletter* 1:5, July 1980.

Derevensky, Jeffrey, and Elaine B. Coleman, "Gifted Children's Fears," *Gifted Child Quarterly* 33:2, Spring 1989.

Rogers, Martin, and Linda Silverman, "Recognizing Giftedness in Young Children," *Understanding Our Gifted*, November 1988.

Chapter 4

Delisle, James R., "Gifted Children's Fears," *Gifted Children Newsletter*, February 1984.

Delisle, Jim, "Preventive Counseling for the Gifted Adolescent: From Words to Action," *Roeper Review* 3:21-25, November/December 1980.

Farrell, Donna M., "Suicide among Gifted Students," *Roeper Review* 11:3:134-139, March 1989.

Greenlaw, M. Jean, and Margaret E. McIntosh, *Educating the Gifted, A Sourcebook* (Chicago: American Library Association, 1988).

Hollingworth, Leta S., *Children above 180 IQ* (New York: Arno Press, 1975).

Schmitz, Connie C., and Judy Galbraith, *Managing the Social and Emotional Needs of the Gifted* (Minneapolis: Free Spirit Publishing Inc., 1985).

Van Tassel-Baska, J., editor, *A Practical Guide to Counseling the Gifted in a School Setting* (Reston, VA: ERIC Clearinghouse for the Gifted, 1983).

Webb, James, Elizabeth Meckstroth, and Stephanie S. Tolan, *Guiding the Gifted Child: A Practical Source for Parents and Teachers* (Columbus, OH: Ohio Psychology Publishing Co., 1982).

Webb, J.T., E.A. Meckstroth, and S.S. Tolan, "Stress Management: Some Specific Suggestions," *The Creative Child and Adult Quarterly* 8:4:217-220, 1983.

Chapter 5

Bruner, J.S., *The Process of Education* (Cambridge, MA: Harvard University Press, 1960).

Galbraith, Judy, *The Gifted Kids Survival Guide (For Ages 11-18)* (Minneapolis: Free Spirit Publishing Inc., 1983).

Maker, C.J., *Curriculum Development for the Gifted* (Rockville, MD: Aspen Systems, 1982).

Renzulli, J., *The Enrichment Triad Model: A Guide for Developing Defensible Programs for the Gifted and Talented* (Mansfield Center, CT: Creative Learning Press, 1977).

VanTassel-Baska, J., *An Administrator's Guide to the Education of Gifted and Talented Children* (Washington, DC: National Association of State Boards of Education, 1981).

Chapter 6

Coleman, Dona, "Parenting the Gifted: Is This a Job for Superparent?" *G/C/T*, March/April 1982.

Ginsberg, G., and C.H. Harrison, *How to Help Your Gifted Child* (New York: Simon & Schuster, 1977).

Knopper, Dorothy, "Profiles and Perspectives," *Roeper Review* 11:4, May 1989.

Mathews, F. Neil, "Influencing Parents' Attitudes Toward Gifted Education," *Exceptional Children* 48:140-42, October 1981.

Steinbach, Trevor T., "State Gifted Advocacy: A Guide for Parents, Teachers, and Coordinators" (Illinois Council for the Gifted, 1981).

Wiess, Patricia, and James Gallagher, "Parental Educational Preferences for Gifted Children," *G/C/T* 30:2-6, November/December 1983.

INDEX

A

Acceleration
  and gifted education, 84
Achievement
  defined, 20
  tests, 20
Activities
  at home, 116-17
Adderholdt-Elliott, Miriam, 77
Adolescence, 40, 120
Adults
  dependency on, 42
Advanced placement
  for high school students, 87
Advocacy
  for better education, 99-114
Advocacy groups, 106
Advocate
  defined, 99
Age
  emotional, intellectual, and physical, 39-40
Allergies
  and learning disabilities, 31
Alvino, James, 55
Amabile, Teresa M., 55
Animals, cruelty to, 71
Anorexia nervosa, 71
Anxiety
  and perfectionism, 67-68
AP classes. *See* Advanced placement
Appearance
  and perfectionism, 67
  preoccupation with, 72
Arguing, 41-42
Armstrong, Thomas, 34
Artistic intelligence
  and identification of giftedness, 24
  suppressed in school, 17
Attention deficit disorder
  of male students, 29-30
Average
  as test score, 18-19

B

Behavior disorders, 79-80
Bell-shaped curve
  of intelligence tests, 18
Bibliotherapy, 47
Bilingual gifted children
  identification of, 32-33

Binet, Alfred
  and intelligence test development, 6
Biographies, 59, 68
Bodily-kinesthetic intelligence
  learning style, 16
Books, 34, 55, 76-77, 97, 114, 125-26
Boredom
  in school, 96, 117
Bray, James
  on gifted education, 11
*Bringing Out the Best: A Resource Guide for
  Parents of Young Gifted Children*
  (Saunders/Espeland), xiii, 125
Bulimia, 71
Burn out
  as myth, 7-8
  of parents, 122
  of super-achievers, 73

C

Calligraphy, 41
Cassidy, Jack
  on early reading skills, 52
*The Centering Book: Awareness Activities for
  Children and Adults to Relax the Body &
  Mind* (Hendricks/Wills), 55
Charlemagne
  and education for gifted children, 5
Checklist
  for identification of giftedness, 21-22
Childish behavior, 40, 63
Clark, Barbara, 34
Coleman, Elaine
  on fears of gifted children, 46
College-level classes, 87
*The Colorado Handbook for Parents of Gifted
  Children* (Gonzales), 30, 97
Compulsive behavior, 73
Computers, 41
Concentration
  and attention span, 48
  on interests, 45
Cooperative learning
  disadvantages of, 18
Cornell, Dewey G.
  on gifted labeling, 27
Council of State Directors of Programs for the
  Gifted, 109
Counseling, 74-76
Creative gifted children
  traits, 23

131

Creativity tests
    and identification of giftedness, 23
Criticism
    positive, 66, 67
Cruelty to animals, 71
Curriculum
    for gifted education, 89-92
    and teacher's role, 94-95
    See also Education, gifted; Schools

D

Danger signs, 70-74
Darwin, Charles
    and theory of evolution, 7
Death
    coping with fear of, 47
    preoccupation with, 74
Decision making, 42
Depression, 74
Derevensky, Jeffrey
    on fears of gifted children, 46
Differentiation
    in gifted education curriculum, 90-92
*Directory of American Youth Organizations: A
    Guide to Over 400 Clubs, Groups, Troops,
    Teams, Societies, Lodges, and More for Young
    People* (Erickson), 76
Disabled gifted children, 31-32
Divergent thinker
    defined, 23
Dropouts, 13
Drug use, 54, 72

E

Eating disorders, 71
Education
    history of, 6
    individualized, 11
Education bills
    legislative process for, 108-09
Education, gifted, 9-14, 79-97, 99-114
    advocacy, 99-114
    changing public opinion about, 5-6, 9-10
    coordinators, 13, 29, 76, 101, 105
    curriculum, 89-92
    differentiation in, 90-92
    and elitism as fallacy, 11
    funding, 12, 13-14, 107-09
    identification of students for, 19-25, 89, 110
    methods of programming, 84-87
    national efforts, 13-14
    parents' comments on, 60, 83, 88, 93, 96
    philosophy statement regarding, 101
    program evaluation, 92
    programming methods, 84-87
    and self-esteem, 60
    state efforts, 11-14, 107-10
    statistics, 12
    See also Curriculum; Schools

Elitism
    of gifted education, 11
    of intelligence tests, 10
Energy levels
    of gifted children, 38
    of male students, 29
Enrichment programs, 85, 86, 121
Environment
    and intelligence, 5, 7
Erickson, Judith B., 76
Eye contact
    and communication, 48

F

Failure. *See* Perfectionism; Risk-taking
Family therapists, 76
Fantasy worlds
    withdrawal into, 73
Fatigue
    and super-achievers, 73
Fears
    of gifted children, 46-47
Federal Department of Education (U.S.)
    and funding for gifted education, 14
*Fighting Invisible Tigers: A Stress Management
    Guide for Teens* (Hipp), 77
*Frames of Mind: The Theory of Multiple
    Intelligences* (Gardner), 16, 34
*Full Flowering: A Parent and Teacher Guide to
    Programs for the Gifted* (Perry), 114
Funding
    for gifted education, 12, 13-14, 107-09

G

Galbraith, Judy, 96, 97
Galton, Francis
    on intelligence and heredity, 7
Gardner, Howard
    on multiple intelligences and learning styles,
        16-17, 34
Genetic Studies of Genius (Terman), 6
Gifted
    on bell-shaped curve, 19
    definitions of, 15-16, 33
    first use of term, 6
    pros and cons of label, 25-28
    state definitions of, 109
Gifted Child Today (periodical), 11
Gifted children
    identification of, 19-25, 89, 110
    labeling, 3, 9, 25-28
    misconceptions about, 9
    traits, 23, 32-33
    See also Bilingual gifted children; Creative gift-
        ed children; Disabled gifted children;
        Minority gifted children; Poor gifted chil-
        dren; Young gifted children
Gifted Children Monthly (periodical), 55
Gifted Children Newsletter (periodical), 52
Gifted/Creative/Talented (periodical), 11
Gifted education. *See* Education, gifted

The Gifted Kids Survival Guides
     (Galbraith/Delisle), xiii, 97
Gifted program coordinator, 13, 29, 76, 101, 105
Golant, Susan K., 55
Gonzalez, Julio, 97
Gordon, Thomas, 77
Gowan, John C.
     on definition of gifted, 16
Grades
     as indication of giftedness, 24
Gripes
     of parents, 3
Group intelligence tests
     and identification of giftedness, 19-20
*Growing Up Creative: Nurturing a Lifetime of
     Creativity* (Amabile), 55
Growing Up Gifted (Clark), 34
Guiding Gifted Readers (Halsted), 125
Guiding the Gifted Child (Webb), 126

H

Halsted, Judith Wynn, 125
Handwriting, 41
Help
     how to get, 74-76
     when to get, 70-74
Hendricks, Gay, 55
Heredity
     and intelligence, 5, 7
Hereditary Genius (Galton), 7
High school students
     gifted education opportunities for, 87
Hipp, Earl, 77
Honesty
     and answers to questions, 37
Honor roll
     as indication of giftedness, 24
How to Parent so Children Will Learn (Rimm), 125
Humor, sense of
     in gifted children, 44
     in parents, 113
Hyperactivity
     vs. activity for a reason, 38

I

Idealism
     about world affairs, 62-63
Illinois
     legislative process for education bills, 108-09,
        110
*In Their Own Way: Discovering and Encouraging
     Your Child's Personal Learning Style*
     (Armstrong), 34
Independence
     of adolescents, 120
Independent study, 87, 90, 92
Individual intelligence tests
     and identification of giftedness, 20
Individualized education, 11
The Inner Voices of a Musical Genius (Oswald), 7
Insanity of Genius (Lombroso), 7

Insurance
     for mental health services, 76
Intelligence
     as biological, 7
     as educable, 6
     and environment, 5, 7
     as fixed, 6
     and heredity, 5, 7
     multiple, 16
     as quantitative, 7-8
Intelligence quotient. *See* IQ
Intelligence tests
     bell-shaped curve of, 18
     as biased against minorities, 11
     development of, 6
     group, 19-20
     and identification of giftedness, 19-20
     individual, 20
     and promotion of elitism, 10
Interests
     and concentration, 45, 48
     and lack of neatness, 50
     and specialization, 45
Internships
     for high school students, 87
Interpersonal intelligence
     learning style, 17
     suppressed in schools, 17
Intrapersonal intelligence
     learning style, 17
     suppressed in schools, 17
IQ
     average, 6
     intimidation by, 118
Isolation
     feelings of, 58
     self-imposed, 70

J

Jacob K. Javits Gifted and Talented Students
        Education Act
     for gifted education funding, 13
Jacobs, Jon
     on identification of giftedness, 20-21
Javits (Jacob K.) Gifted and Talented Students
        Education Act
     for gifted education funding, 13
Jefferson, Thomas
     on equality, 10
     and university education for gifted youth, 5
*Journal of the American Academy of Child and
     Adolescent Psychiatry*, 71
The Joys and Challenges of Raising a Gifted Child
     (Golant), 55

K

Kaufman, Gershen, 77
Kennedy, John F.
     and development of potential, 10
Klene, Richard R.
     on alleviating fears, 47

Knopper, Dorothy
    and advocacy for gifted education, 100

L

Labeling
    childrens' feelings about, 27
    of gifted children, 3, 9
    parents' feelings about, 28
    pros and cons of, 25-28
League of Women Voters, 110
Learning disabilities, 31-32
Learning environment
    in gifted education curriculum, 90-92
Learning styles
    of children, 16-17
Legislators
    letters to, 108, 110-12
    telephone calls to, 108, 110, 113
Letters
    to legislators, 108, 110-12
    samples, 111-12
Libraries
    and gifted education, 85
Linguistic intelligence
    learning style, 16
Logical-mathematical intelligence
    learning style, 16
Lombroso, Cesare
    on linkage of genius with psychiatric disorders, 7

M

*Managing the Social and Emotional Needs of the
    Gifted* (Schmitz/Galbraith), 97
Manual dexterity, 41
Marland Report, 12-13
Memory, 38
Mensa, 59
Mental Health Association, 76
Mentally disabled
    on bell-shaped curve, 19
Mentorships
    and gifted education, 87
Michigan
    gifted education in, 100
Minority gifted children
    identification of, 32-33
Misconceptions
    about gifted children, 9
Mistakes, 68, 69
Mood problems
    and creative people, 7
Motivation, 24, 45
Motor skills, 41
Musical intelligence
    learning style, 16
Myths
    about giftedness, 7-8

N

Narcissism, 72
National Achievement Scholarship Program, 11
National Association for Gifted Children
    and national program for gifted, 13
National Association of Anorexia Nervosa and
    Associated Disorders, Inc., 77
National Research Center on the Gifted and
    Talented, 14
National State Leadership Institute, 11
Neatness, 50-52
Nichols, Michael P., 77

O

Obnoxious behavior, 121-22
Observation
    learning by, 39, 43
Office of Education (U.S.)
    definition of gifted, 16
    studies on programs for gifted, 10, 12
Office of the Gifted (U.S.)
    and state plans for gifted education, 11
Organization
    of childrens' belongings, 51-52
Oswald, Peter
    on relationship of creative/talented lifestyle
        and mood problems, 7
Overeating, 72

P

Parents
    burn out, 122
    and diplomacy, 103
    on gifted education, 60, 83, 88, 93, 96
    on gifted teachers, 95
    gripes of, 3
    and identification of giftedness, 21-22, 25, 29,
        31
    insecurities of, 122
    and positive comments, 67
    questions asked by, 115-23
    and school involvement, 2, 25, 29, 70, 81, 89,
        92, 94, 95, 99-114
    staying in touch, 53-54
    support for, 105, 107, 122
A Parent's Guide to Eating Disorders (Valette), 77
*Parents' Guide to Raising a Gifted Child:
    Recognizing and Developing Your Child's
    Potential* (Alvino), 55
Parents' Guide to Raising a Gifted Toddler
    (Alvino), 55
Peers
    and identification of giftedness, 24
    and pressure to be similar, 40, 54, 58, 82
Perfectionism, 64-69
    extreme, 70
    and risk-taking, 65
Perfectionism: What's Bad About Being Too Good?
    (Adderholdt-Elliott), 77
Periodicals, 126

Perry, Phyllis J., 114
Perry, Susan K., 55
Physical activity
    as addicting, 48
    and energy levels, 38
    examples, 48
    and motor skills, 41
    need for, 47-48, 117
Plato
    as advocate for gifted children, 5
*Playing Smart: A Parent's Guide to Enriching,
    Offbeat Learning Activities for Ages 4-14*
    (Perry), 55
Poor gifted children
    identification of, 33
The Power of the Family (Nichols), 77
Praise, 66
Preschool years, 40
Priority setting, 69
Private schools
    vs. public, 120-21
Problems
    coping with, 57-77
    signs of, 70-74
Process
    as important part of learning, 90, 119
Procrastination
    and perfectionism, 65
Psychiatric social workers, 76
Psychiatrists, 76
Psychologists, 76
Public schools
    vs. private, 120-21
Pull-out programs
    and gifted education, 86

Q

Questions
    asked by gifted children, 36-37, 63
    asked by parents, 115-23
    without answers, 43, 115

R

Readiness, 39, 52
Reading, 52, 117, 118
Recommended reading
    books, 34, 55, 76-77, 97, 114, 125-26
    periodicals, 126
Reference books
    as source of answers to childrens' questions,
    37
Relaxation
    need for, 48-50
    techniques, 50
Religious beliefs, 63
Renzulli, Joseph
    on definition of gifted, 16
    on motivation, 24
Resource rooms
    and gifted education, 85

Richardson Foundation
    gifted education survey, 13
Rigid behavior, 73
Rimm, Sylvia, 125
Risk-taking
    importance of, 43
    and perfectionism, 65
Roberts, Gail C., 77

S

Sarcasm, 44
Saunders, Jacqulyn, 125
Schmitz, Connie, 97
School boards
    working with, 104-05
Schools
    and average students, 18-19
    and bored students, 96, 117
    and identification of giftedness, 19-24, 119
    and language skills, 17
    and mathematics skills, 17
    and parent involvement, 2, 25, 29, 70, 81, 89,
    92, 94, 95, 99-114
    programs for gifted in, 10, 12, 16
    public vs. private, 120-21
    student comments on, 96
    See also Curriculum; Education, gifted;
    Teachers
Schumann, Robert
    as musical genius, 7
*The Second Centering Book: More Awareness
    Activities for Children and Adults to Relax the
    Body & Mind* (Hendricks/Roberts), 55
Self
    preoccupation with, 72
Self-esteem
    and differences, 61
    and eating disorders, 71
    and gifted education, 60
    and risk-taking, 43
    and social skills, 58, 59, 64
Sensitivity, heightened, 49, 61-63
Sex-role stereotyping
    and female student ability, 30-31
Siblings, 118-19
Silly behavior, 40
Sleep patterns, 38, 49
Smart Kids with School Problems (Vail), 126
Smutny, Joan Franklin, 125
Social skills, 58-59, 64
Social workers, psychiatric, 76
Society
    as contributing to instability of gifted people, 7
Socioeconomics
    and influence on personality differences, 8
Spatial intelligence
    learning style, 16
Special education directors, 101
Specialists
    at early age, 45
Sputnik
    and increase in science education funding, 10

Standard achievement tests, 20
Stanford-Binet Intelligence Scale, 6, 15
State efforts
    for gifted education, 11-14, 107-09
*Stick Up For Yourself! Every Kid's Guide to Personal
    Power and Positive Self-Esteem*
    (Kaufman/Raphael), 77
Stress
    and perfectionism, 68
Students
    comments on gifted teachers, 94
    identification of giftedness, 24
Substance abuse, 72
Suicide, 74
Super-achievers, 73
Support groups
    for parents, 105, 107, 122
The Survival Guide for Adolescence series
    (Roberts/Guttormson), 77

T

Talented
    definitions of, 16, 33
    state definitions of, 109
Talking
    at early age, 39
Tape recorder
    for dictation of ideas, 41, 49
Task commitment, 24
Teachers
    and awareness of importance for gifted
        education, 14
    and identification of giftedness, 20-21, 25, 29,
        32, 33
    parent comments on, 95
    role, 94-95
    student comments on, 94
    talking with, 101-03
*Teaching Children Self-Discipline at Home and at
    School* (Gordon), 77
Teen years, 40
Telephone calls
    to legislators, 108, 110, 113
    sample, 113
Terman, Lewis
    on burn out as fallacy, 8
    on cause of lazy work habits, 19
    on definition of gifted, 15
    on positive attributes of gifted people, 8
    on stability of gifted people, 7
    and standardized intelligence test, 6
    and use of term "gifted," 6
Testing methods
    and identification of giftedness, 19-20, 23, 89
    types of, 19-20, 23
    See also Intelligence tests
Therapists, family, 76
Therapy. *See* Counseling
Thinking skills
    in gifted education curriculum, 90-92
Tracking. *See* Labeling

Traits
    of gifted children, 23, 32-33
Trust
    and decision making ability, 42
    of promises made, 38

U

The Underachievement Syndrome (Rimm), 125
Underachievers
    as gifted, 20
    how to help, 115-16
    and perfectionism, 65
    in school, 81, 82
Unfinished projects, 46
University of Connecticut at Storrs
    and gifted education, 14
Unwind time, 49

V

Vail, Priscilla, 126
Valette, Brett, 77
Verbal skills
    and identification of giftedness, 32
    and logic, 41
Violence
    unusual fascination with, 71
Vocabulary skills, 39
Vukelich, Carol
    on early reading skills, 52

W

Walking
    at early age, 39
Warning signs, 70-74
Webb, James, 126
Witty, Paul
    on definition of gifted, 15-16
    on programs for gifted, 10
Wordplay, 44
World affairs
    concerns about, 46-47, 62-63
    idealism about, 62-63
    powerlessness and, 70-71
Worries
    of gifted children, 46-47

Y

Young gifted children
    identification of, 33
    and school, 82
Your Gifted Child (Smutny/Veenker/Veenker),
    125

ABOUT THE AUTHOR

SALLY YAHNKE WALKER has a Master's Degree in Guidance and Counseling and has done post-graduate work in Gifted Education, Guidance, Early Childhood, and Parent Education. Currently, as coordinator of Gifted Services at Education Service Center #1 in Rockford, Illinois, she helps school districts implement gifted programming and does teacher training. She has also taught identified gifted children and worked as a Parent Educator for the parents of those in gifted programs.

After working with parent groups for ten years, she has found that parents of the gifted and talented are full of questions and hungry for information about their children. As a parent of three teenagers herself, she can readily relate to the joys and frustrations of parenting.